YOU TOO Can Be DELIVERED

Keys to Walking in Personal Deliverance

William E. Dickerson II

YOU TOO
Can Be
DELIVERED

Keys to Walking in
Personal Deliverance

YOU TOO CAN BE DELIVERED: Keys to Walking in Personal Deliverance

To contact the author for speaking engagements or deliverance meetings, call 617-740-9482.

ISBN: 0-924748-47-8
UPC: 88571300017-8

Printed in the United States of America
© 2005 by William E. Dickerson II

Cover by: Tony Laidig, www.thirstydirt.com

Milestones International Publishers
4410 University Drive, Ste. 113
Huntsville, AL 35816
(256) 536-9402, ext. 234; Fax: (256) 536-4530
www.milestonesinternationalpublishers.com

1 2 3 4 5 6 7 8 9 10 / 10 09 08 07 06 05

Endorsements

꙳꙳

"Dickerson's perspective on 'deliverance' is the most profound view I've read on the subject in a long time. The book reaches down to the common man with a message that it's not how you start, but more importantly how you finish. God bless the messenger!"

—Bishop Wiley Jackson Jr.
Senior Pastor, Gospel Tabernacle Church
Chief Apostle of the Word In Action
Fellowship of Pastors, Atlanta, Georgia

"Thank God for Pastor Dickerson, who has taken the time to inform, encourage and challenge all of us to understand what true deliverance is all about. Wrapped around definitions, the graphic testimonies he provides are of people who have been supernaturally delivered from the handiwork of Satan by the power of God. This is a must-read for all ministers."

—Dr. Wanda A. Turner
Author, Teacher, Preacher

"I am delighted to know that there are still yielded vessels bringing Christ's message of deliverance to the captives. Pastor Dickerson embodies such an individual, one who is willing to go into the trenches to see that the least of the brethren will have an opportunity to hear the Gospel message of the kingdom. This book should be used by anyone who is serious about being delivered or helping people to receive their deliverance."

—Bishop LeRoy Bailey Jr.
Senior Pastor, The First Cathedral, Bloomfield, Connecticut
Author, *A Solid Foundation:*
Building Your Life From the Ground Up

"There are very few men who speak about the litigious topic of deliverance with such ebullience as Pastor William Dickerson. His passion to see people delivered from the oppressive bonds of demonic oppression is evident in everything he does. That same passion can be felt ever so fervently when you read his outstanding work, *You Too Can Be Delivered.* If per chance you have ever doubted God's awesome power to deliver the vilest soul, this book is necessary reading for you. I am thoroughly convinced that after you read this work that not only will you believe that God can deliver anyone, but also that it is very possible you too can be delivered."

—Bishop Noel Jones
Senior Pastor, City of Refuge, Gardena, California

This book was written in memory of a rare treasure and amazing servant of God. She was the quintessential essence of what true holiness and servant leadership is about. She was my mentor, confidante and friend; my mother, the late Rev. Alma Dickerson (1929 – 1978).

Table of Contents

Table of Contents

Continued

Acknowledgments

First and foremost, I give glory to my Lord and Savior, Jesus the Christ. This book was written through the strength and spiritual guidance given to me by my heavenly Father. To Him I am eternally indebted. To my lovely wife, Luella, who has supported me throughout our 24 years of marriage; Luella personifies the characteristics of a virtuous woman. For this, I am blessed. To each of my children: William III, Kyanna, Latia and Kevin. You've taught me more about myself and helped me develop as a father, servant and leader.

I would like to thank Pastor Samuel B. Hogan Sr. for giving me a solid biblical foundation and for teaching me how to be a man of integrity and the importance of practical holiness. Pastor Hogan's teachings have assisted me to have a very balanced theological perspective on ministry. My biblical upbringing under his leadership within the Church Of God In Christ (COGIC) has made an indelible mark upon my family and me. During my formative years as a new minister under Pastor Hogan is when I had on-the-job training in deliverance ministry.

I want to thank Bishop Wiley Jackson Jr. for his invaluable advice over the years and for encouraging me to think outside the box. He leads with much determination and excellence. I also want to thank Bishop Hester Bordeaux for his leadership and concern for me. His saintly and profound influence helped us to facilitate our church's latest building acquisition. Thanks and appreciation to Elder William Tate, my childhood friend and confidant; he has been a constant encourager over the years.

Thanks and humble gratitude to Pastor Keith Young, a trustworthy adviser and friend. He has challenged me in positive ways, which have been God-sent. Thanks to Pastor Rogers Murray for his friendship and consistent support. In addition I thank and appreciate my son in the Gospel, Apostle Adam Gaines, his wife, Valerie, and the Anointed Light Church family for their prayers and support.

Much appreciation goes to the church that I am fortunate to pastor, the Greater Love Tabernacle Church family. Thank you for your continued prayerful support throughout the duration of our spiritual journey together. I'm especially grateful to those courageous souls who freely shared their testimonies in this book; I truly believe that their candid stories will impact generations to come. I also thank each person who assisted me in the completion of this book. Also special thanks to Sister Davi Chandrasekaren (husband Dr. Shiva) for proofreading this text and to Minister Barbara Dulin for continually handling my busy schedule. Last but not least, with profound elation I thank my brother in the Lord, Aaron D. Lewis and his wife, Tiwanna, and the Family of God Church. Thank you, Aaron, for challenging me to write this book. And, to you I write, "Yes, it is done!"

Foreword

Deliverance is a mindset and an ongoing process for any individual seeking to be set free from his or her cycle of bondage. Often the word *deliverance* as understood within Christian circles is accompanied by a negative connotation of mysterious rituals that can only be unraveled by those who are privileged enough to have some type of "secretive" power and authority with God.

You Too Can Be Delivered is a timely message and vital word to anyone who has ever asked the question, "How can I be set free from the yoke of bondage that hinders my daily walk?" Having operated in deliverance ministry for over 20 years, I know firsthand the decisive and subtle tactics that the enemy uses to impede the progress of God in our lives.

Quite often I tell my congregation that just because you stop doing something does not necessarily mean that you are delivered from it. It could simply mean that you just lack opportunity. With that in mind, one must look at deliverance as an ongoing process of spiritual cleansing. In these profound messages of deliverance, Pastor Dickerson confronts many questions regarding this controversial topic. His many years of experience, divine encounters and the Spirit of God operating through him, will all help to shed some much-needed light regarding a person's ability to walk in total freedom from the bondage of Satan's devices. This work also will serve as a how-to manual on maintaining one's deliverance.

Ritualistic efforts will never produce ongoing freedom in a believer's life. You must rather maintain an ongoing relationship with the Lord and allow the Spirit of God to be your guide if you really desire to be free. As Pastor Dickerson so boldly states in this profound text, "You don't have to hide your sins or struggles any longer. Christ can set you free."

My prayer is that as you delve into the depths of this spiritual warfare tool that you will be empowered. Use this tool as an instrument of survival, not simply as mere entertainment. As Pastor Dickerson dispels the myths and reveals the truth concerning the power of God to deliver and set the captives free, I trust that the Word of the Lord will minister also to your soul and give you the courage to break free forever.

Bishop George Bloomer
Senior Pastor of Bethel Family Worship Center Church,
Durham, NC
Best-selling Author: *Witchcraft in the Pews:
Who's Sitting next to You*
and *Spiritual Warfare*

Introduction

I can clearly remember worship services being abruptly disrupted at the small storefront church in Boston, Massachusetts, that I frequented as a child with my mother. Grown women and young girls suddenly and mysteriously fell to the floor as if struck down by lightning. Instead of shouting about the goodness of God, they shrieked and shouted words in strange tongues. Their soft feminine voices became increasingly more baritone as sounds of demons roared from within them.

Sensing a need to deal with this unexpected change, the pastor of the church would immediately call for a deliverance service. The faithful parishioners sensed such urgency in his voice that they instinctively, as if they were soldiers on call, surrounded these women and brought them to the front of the church to the altar for prayer. Knowing that the next series of events would be far too R-rated for most children to handle, the ushers on duty hurriedly escorted the children to the back of the church or into another room altogether to ensure that they would not have a clear view of what was about to happen.

Having been trained well by the example of deliverance ministers, all the saints knew that it was time to call on Jesus and summon His presence. They knew that only God had the power to drive out the evil spirits living inside these women. So they leaned heavily on His power, calling on His Name until their deliverance manifested.

From the back of the church I heard people crying out, "Jesus, Jesus, Jesus." They called on the Name of the Lord seemingly for hours.

They would not cease from calling on the Name of Jesus until the possessed women and girls were set free from the clutches of demonic oppression and possession. It went from one extreme to the other. At first I heard them speaking with a demonic tone as they spewed out bedeviled words. Then I heard these same people begin to unashamedly and unrestrainedly offer God the most amazing praises with their tongues. Deliverance had surely come!

They truly received their deliverance, but simply being "delivered" was not enough for us Holy Spirit-filled believers. We wanted to make sure that these spirits would not return and that the "once possessed persons" would not fall into some kind of regressive behavior. The only panacea that we knew of was the baptism in the Holy Spirit. We believed that if a person was filled with the Holy Spirit, it was very unlikely for any other kind of foreign spirit to live in the same body simultaneously with the Holy Spirit. One of the spirits would inevitably have to vacate the premises. And surely the Holy Spirit would take priority over any lesser spirits.

The congregation patiently waited for God to fill the formerly demon-possessed women with His Holy Spirit. Back then I didn't really understand what I do now about this controversial topic known as deliverance. My mother, Reverend Alma Dickerson, who was an anointed evangelist in her own right, informed me after these services exactly what was going on. She told me that the loud noises I heard coming from inside those women and sometimes girls were evil spirits or demons. As a small child, I found it quite intriguing that an evil spirit could use someone else's voice to speak. It was kind of like a ventriloquist's act, a sort of Charlie McCarthy and Edgar Bergen show. I thought it was pretty cool. But on the other hand, it also scared me beyond measure.

Even as I grew older, my childhood memories of these events, of how these women spoke and how they behaved never escaped me. My belief in a God who was able to deliver people from demons and addictions grew more and more. I learned that the forces of darkness that battle against the forces of light could inhabit anyone who has not been protected by the Blood of Jesus the Christ.

What happened in this small storefront church during the late 1960s and early 1970s was a special milestone for me. It was far more than a passing scene from a movie or a good chapter in a Stephen King horror book. These experiences served as the infrastructure on which I later built a ministry of deliverance and restoration that freed thousands of people from their private cellblocks of hopelessness and despair.

As an eight-year-old little boy, it was really difficult for me to understand the concept of angels, demons, deliverance and witchcraft. I clearly saw visions, but I could not label what I had seen until an older person, far wiser than I, was able to explain these things to me. Although they did the best that they could in giving their coined explanations, their reasoning did not satisfy my voracious appetite for wanting to know more about this liberating subject.

At times I attended horror flicks in an inquisitive effort to do my own investigation. Those scary pictures increased my childish imagination. When I thought of the devil, I imagined a great, big, beastly looking guy with hooves and horns whose flesh was indecently exposed. I saw this ghastly caricature wielding a scorching hot pitchfork and dragging around a long thick tail. I suppose my image of the devil was not far from the common depictions of the devil seen in Hollywood movies.

I did not clearly understand what all this stuff meant, why demons roamed around in susceptible persons. It made far less sense to me why a demon showed up during a deliverance service or even in a deliverance church for that matter, knowing that there would be a serious showdown with a pretty major possibility of losing. I figured that the devil was a glutton for agonizing punishment. At least that is what my childlike mind contemplated. The whole agenda became increasingly perplexing. However, that only led me to begin seeking out answers to all of my bewildering questions about deliverance.

"If demons are inside of people, then how did they get there?" This greatly concerned me because if evil spirits could easily get into other people, it just might be possible that they could get ahold of the people whom I loved most, and possibly even me! "If the preacher had the power to call the demons out of someone, was it possible for me to actually see one?" I actually wanted to see how a demon looked. Maybe if I knew exactly how they looked, I would be able to identify them early on, ending their destructive patterns—or so I thought.

"Could demons actually manifest themselves in a natural form? If so, what types of forms could they take on?" Maybe demons could show up in animals, I thought. As I got older and began to understand more about the Word of God, I realized that my suspicions were very realistic. I read that two men from the Gadarene region were demon possessed and that when they saw Jesus they immediately recognized not only who He was but also His power and authority. When Jesus cast the demons out of these possessed men, the demons went into the pigs by their (the demons') own request.

> *Some distance from them a large herd of pigs was feeding. The demons begged Jesus, "If you drive us out, send us into the herd of pigs." He said to them, "Go!" So they came out and went into the pigs, and the whole herd rushed down the steep bank into the lake and died in the water* (Matthew 8:30-32).

So full of queries, I was really intrigued by this possibility of actually seeing a demon or demons. "If the demon is angry, would it try to hurt me or one of my siblings?" During those days, my mother told me that if I was filled with the Holy Spirit I didn't need to worry about whether a demon would possess me or not. She boldly informed me, "When those demons try to come against you, they will have to back up since you have surrendered yourself totally to the Lord." What I came to realize is that demons inhabit people who will give them the least resistance—the weak and feeble-minded folks. If I were living right, then they'd try to find someone else far easier to catch.

My mother gave me very strict teachings about the importance of true holiness. True holiness to me was not about "do's and don'ts." I was taught about who I was in relationship to God and His awesome power working in me. Holiness was about the manifestation of the Holy Spirit in my life, being able to cast out evil spirits and lay hands on sick people and see them recover.

When I was young, I used to believe that the door to repentance was a very narrow opening that few would ever make it through. My religious teachers drilled into me that if I sinned I'd go straight to hell. Although I now understand God's grace on a far more mature level than I did then, I am still very thankful for those strict holiness lessons. I learned a very fundamental lesson: I couldn't play with God; I had to be real.

Everything that I know about deliverance today is a direct outgrowth of my childhood experiences, which served as a foundation for my intimate walk with God. Both then and now, I use those experiences as my frame of reference since I witnessed firsthand so many strange things happening to church people during worship services. One memory that I could never forget is going to hear the well-known evangelist Reverend R.W. Schambach with my mother when I was about nine or ten years old. I remember what happened just as clear as day.

At this particular revival service, a demon-possessed man suddenly fell out in the aisle while the worship service was in progress. My mother and other Christians gathered around him to pray for him, asking God to set him free from demonic forces. This was no easy chore as the demons inside him vehemently opposed them and their prayers. The man began fighting and resisting their goodly efforts and then began spewing out curse words to God. I couldn't believe that this man was actually cursing in a church service. It was like watching a Hollywood movie as I watched his face turn different colors.

He began limping around the church looking real evil. Then without any notice, his deliverance began to happen. Slowly, yet right in front of our eyes, we began to see this insane-looking man begin to appear quite rational. The saints kept on praying and praising God, knowing that they could not cease doing either until this man's deliverance was totally complete. The man clumsily fell down, then managed to get back up and then started to run around the auditorium.

His once discolored face was returning to his original caramel-colored skin complexion. His face was no longer deformed, evil-looking or distorted at all. He walked around like a dignified man. Even his limp was gone. He began to talk very coherently. Beyond any doubt, I knew then that the ministry of deliverance was very real. And that conviction would only grow as the years continued.

In my nearly 24 years of ministry, I've seen demons manifest in various ways. And these experiences, coupled with God's Word, have caused me to come to some remarkable conclusions about this subject. One thing I have discovered is that there are times when Christians can be saved, but may still need to be delivered from certain things in their lives. Based on my studies of the Bible, I do not believe that Christians can be demon-possessed. However, I do believe that they can yield themselves to certain demonic activities.

Christians can expose themselves to things that will cause an open door for Satan to enter. Once he enters in he begins to set up shop within the individual, ultimately planning to destroy him or her. The stories presented in this book are true stories that offer the reader hope of being free once and for all. It does not matter how long you have dealt with a particular problem, habit or sin; everyone can be delivered by the power of Christ if he has a genuine desire to be free and the willingness to take massive action to make it come to pass.

Although each person has a major role to play in his or her own deliverance process, deliverance is not solely on the shoulders of the individual. Christ Himself has taken on the major role, the larger part, by giving Himself as a human sacrifice in exchange for your deliverance. Many believers understand the concept of Christ's sacrificial death as it relates to our salvation. Others have graduated to seize the reality of this same sacrifice as the basis for all healing—emotional, mental and physical. Few, though, have actualized the promise of deliverance as produced by that initial sacrifice.

Unfortunately the church has not been as active as she could have been throughout the years in informing people of the truth: "You don't have to hide your sins or struggle in sin any longer; Christ can set you free." This message is the fundamental message that I have preached during my entire ministry. I was reared as a young minister in a solid church. Those of us who believe in the power of deliverance have a great modern legacy that was left behind by such great spiritual stalwarts as Bishop Charles Harrison Mason, the COGIC founding father who died in 1961.

I have seen countless conversions and witnessed firsthand thousands of people being delivered from drug addiction, homosexuality, sexual compulsiveness, alcoholism, schizophrenia, cigarette chain-smoking and spirits of fear and hatred. I am even more convinced today that every believer can walk in the freedom that Christ has made possible for us.

In each story you will experience vicariously what it feels like to be bound, but far greater than that, what it feels like to be free. I have personally ministered to many people who simply would not believe that God could actually deliver them. They falsely believed that their sin was far too strong for God to destroy. Many others did not believe that God could actually forgive them of their sins, as if God holds lasting grudges against people.

Each story will dispel those fallacies. If you truly desire to be free and stay free, this book is for you. You may be presently walking in victory in your spiritual walk with God and believe that this book is not for you. Not so, for as Christians we are called to be missionaries to the foreign soils of our brothers' and sisters' souls. With that in mind, this book will be a valued resource and guide on how to help someone else receive his or her deliverance.

After Part One, which details personal testimonies, I have listed in Part Two a simple nine-step approach to deliverance. Although this may not be the most comprehensive list available, it is the one that has successfully worked for me and the people whom I have ministered to time and again. I sincerely believe that if you apply each step, you will experience similar victory. As with anything, you can never expect more than you are willing to contribute. Realize, though, that you are not in this fight alone. Jesus the Christ is fighting with you, giving you everything that you will ever need to conquer the devil now and for eternity.

So if the Son sets you free, you will be free indeed (John 8:36).

The sting of death is sin, and the power of sin is the law. But thanks be to God! He gives us the victory through our Lord Jesus Christ (1 Corinthians 15:56-57).

Preface

What Is Deliverance?

＊＊＊

Prior to the first section, I thought it would be well needed to explain what deliverance actually is. Deliverance means a lot of different things to different people. Some ministers believe that they have participated in a deliverance service or experience if they have simply encountered a peak state of emotionalism. Others feel deliverance has come if they witness people crying out loudly, screaming, violently shaking or at times even vomiting.

Although these characteristics may be a byproduct of a person's deliverance, those things alone are not deliverance. In short, deliverance always comes to fulfill a mission. That mission is to set people free. So if a person experiences all the outward expressions mentioned above yet at the end of that experience is still bound by the addiction or compulsion that gripped his or her soul, that person is simply not delivered.

He or she may have experienced the most incredible feeling. Feelings, however, are not the intended goal; freedom is. Consider the Jewish Holocaust in Europe or the African slavery in the United States. Neither the Jews nor the African people would have ever considered it fair or rewarding if they only experienced an incredible feeling of freedom and not freedom itself. The enemy will often cause you to focus on the wrong things rather than on what is right. Jesus is the Deliverer. Everyone whom He delivers is truly free.

Now the Lord is the Spirit, and where the Spirit of the Lord is, there is freedom (2 Corinthians 3:17).

So what is the meaning of deliverance? Deliverance means "a ransom in full." It means to be free. It means to be rid of the sins that hold you down. It also means salvation. Deliverance means redemption as well as to be free and forgiven. However, for the sake of clarity, I would like to define deliverance as "the act or progressive process of being set free from demonic and carnal influences, addictive behaviors, sinful habits and the power of control." Quite naturally any person who needs to be delivered would want to receive his or her deliverance instantaneously. However, deliverance is not always immediate. Deliverance can take place right away or it can take place gradually.

When one is delivered, often he or she will go through a process of being set free. Some people argue that if God does not deliver you instantaneously then it is not authentic. That train of thought is inconsistent with the Scriptures. There is an account in the Bible in the book of Luke when Jesus healed men who had a disease called leprosy.

Leprosy was a disease that affected not just the physical but also the mental and emotional realms.

Lepers were quarantined to their own private communities, away from the rest of civil society. They were removed from their families and friends as they were deemed ceremonially unclean and social outcasts. So their healing required deliverance also. They needed to be set free from the implications of their sickness and struggle. When Jesus healed them, they were not healed in an instant but rather "as they went." That implies that deliverance is a progressive act. This progressive pattern is a good thing in that it teaches valuable lessons from the Father about patience, His grace and divine timing. Not understanding any of those things will cause one to lose what God has given him or her altogether.

Total deliverance is when one is able to walk in complete victory without his or her life being interrupted by the past demonic attacks or influences that had one bound. When one has total deliverance, he or she can walk in bold victory not having to worry about being pulled backward into bondage by former vices.

Some people falsely believe that if they are tempted they need deliverance. That is untrue. Temptation does not mean that you are bound by something. Temptation is simply an indicator that you are human, that you are still encompassed by flesh and bones. Temptation is an indication that you will always have a total dependency on the Father. Jesus was tempted in the wilderness. The Bible goes even further to say that Jesus was *"tempted in every way, just as we are."* Obviously, He had no need to be delivered. The major distinction between Him and us is that Jesus *"yet was without sin."*

> *For we do not have a high priest who is unable to sympathize with our weaknesses, but we have one who has been tempted in every way, just as we are— yet was without sin. Let us then approach the throne of grace with confidence, so that we may receive mercy and find grace to help us in our time of need* (Hebrews 4:15-16).

When we are drawn toward lust, then sin begins to enter in. It is possible to walk in total deliverance. However, the person who desires to be set free must be honest about his or her weaknesses. Do you remember the name Clark Kent? Well, he was the unassuming person who became Superman whenever someone needed supernatural assistance. When Superman performed great feats and courageous acts for people, seemingly nothing could stop him. I was fascinated watching him on TV as a child because he seemed almost invincible.

Although Superman seemed unstoppable, there was one thing that could impede his progress every time, a molten substance called kryptonite. Kryptonite was stronger than Superman and would always drain his power if he came into close proximity with this material. From a spiritual perspective, many of us have a type of "kryptonite" holding us back. In other words, at times we may point at somebody and say that person has a problem with drugs, with sexual addiction, or hatred.

What we often fail to realize is that our own problems can hinder us in our walk with God just as easily as the other person's problem. It is easy to say we are delivered when we have not been tempted. We can stay completely away from things that tempt us, much like Superman stayed away from kryptonite. But can you pass the test in the face of your temptation? Can you say no to sin when it is as tempting as can be? Can you conquer your kryptonite in the form of addiction, perversion, lying, cheating or stealing? If you cannot conquer it, unfortunately it will inevitably conquer you.

The reason so many of us yield to the sins that tempt us is because of lack of proper prayer. When people have not learned to build themselves up in prayer they will be a prime target for the enemy to destroy them. But we cannot judge them as we have been inclined to do so quickly before. We are bound by God's Word to help them and guide them and not criticize them.

One of the things that the enemy will often do is cause people who need to be delivered to live in a state of denial. They will continue to deny that they need help although the need is very evident. One might ask the question: "How do I know I need to be delivered?" Well, it's quite simple to know if you need to be delivered. If you have bad habits or "personal" vices that are holding you back from achieving your highest purpose in God, then you need deliverance.

What exactly is a habit? *Habit* comes from the Latin word *habere*, which means to have. A habit is a thing done often and hence easily. It is a usual way of doing something. It is an addiction, plain and simple. Sometimes people can be addicted to drinking sodas and alcohol. That habit becomes an addiction. It's something that they can't pull away from. It is a natural manner of living for them.

Some people have a bad habit of lying. No matter how hard they try, it seems so hard for them to tell the truth. The more consistently they tell lies, the easier it is for them to keep on lying. Often, demonic influences can encourage us to lie. It is very vital for us to tell the truth because truth exemplifies Godly character. One of the devil's main attributes is that he is a liar. In fact, the Scriptures declare that the devil is the father of lies. In other words, every time you lie, it is because the devil planted the seed of a lie within you. Lies promote the producer of lies, the devil himself. The good news is that the Spirit of Truth can abort the seed of lies.

If you love me, you will obey what I command. And I will ask the Father, and he will give you another Counselor to be with you forever—the Spirit of truth. The world cannot accept him, because it neither sees him nor knows him. But you know him, for he lives with you and will be in you (John 14:15-17).

If we're not cautious, we can claim salvation yet still have problems with lying. In Colossians 3:9 the apostle Paul said, "Lie not" (KJV). He was talking to the church at Colossus. "Stop lying!" This explicitly lets us know that there were some believers involved in the practice of lying. As believers, we must reject any temptation to lie or to operate in a realm that does not promote the truth. The reason for this is that lying can be an open door for even more sinful activity to enter into the soul.

God dealt harshly at the beginning of the early church with a husband and wife named Ananias and Sapphira because they consciously lied to the apostles. God viewed their lie to the apostles as if they lied directly to Him. As a result of their lying spirit God punished them with death. Their story is detailed in the book of the Acts of the Apostles.

Now a man named Ananias, together with his wife Sapphira, also sold a piece of property. With his wife's full knowledge he kept back part of the money for himself, but brought the rest and put it at the apostles' feet. Then Peter said, "Ananias, how is it that Satan has so filled your heart that you have lied to the Holy Spirit and have kept for yourself some of the money you received for the land? Didn't it belong to you before it was sold? And after it was sold, wasn't the money at your disposal? What made you think of doing such a thing? You have not lied to men but to God." When Ananias heard this, he fell down and died. And great fear seized all who heard what had happened. Then the young men came forward, wrapped up his body, and carried him out and buried him. About three hours later his wife came in, not knowing what had happened. Peter asked her, "Tell me, is this the price you and Ananias got for the land?" "Yes," she said, "that is the price." Peter said to her, "How could you agree to test the Spirit of the Lord? Look! The feet of the men who buried your husband are at the door, and they will carry you out also." At that moment she fell down at his feet and died. Then the young men came in and, finding her dead, carried her out and buried her beside her husband. Great fear seized the whole church and all who heard about these events (Acts 5:1-11).

In the days that we live a myriad of issues, problems and sins have inundated our world, far more than can be listed in this section. There are people who may need deliverance from lying, fear or cheating. Some might need deliverance from alcoholism, drug abuse, pornography, guilt and anger. There are various bad habits from which people need deliverance.

For example, perhaps you need to be delivered from alcoholism. No matter what you have tried, you just can't seem to stop drinking. You fully realize that continuing to drink alcohol will eventually destroy everything in your life. Every time you drink alcohol it dulls your sensibility and causes you not to think coherently. The first stride toward your deliverance if you're plagued by alcoholism is to say with a heartfelt conviction, "I want to be set free." You must realize and then say, "I need to be delivered from alcoholism. I'm abusing alcohol and I need to be set free." This is the very first step, recognizing your sin.

For example, many alcoholics lose their families, their jobs and their businesses. More often, these same people do not wake up to the reality of what is going on until they have hit rock bottom. If you're one of those persons who need sdeliverance from a particular stronghold, believe me when I tell you that you don't have to wait until you hit rock bottom. My primary reason for writing this book is to offer you an additional hope. Because I too have been delivered from various addictions, I wanted you to know from a person who has been there that there is a way out.

There are times when men need to be delivered from adultery or fornication. They have what seems like an insatiable lust for women. Medical practitioners and psychiatrists have labeled them as "sexaholics." We must be careful not to continue labeling certain sins as sicknesses and diseases. When we do that, it gives us an excuse to remain the way we are. If we remain the same, we will never receive the deliverance that we so desperately need.

Deliverance is not limited to the outward; it also very often includes the inner challenges such as spirits of depression and fear. And of course, these issues are not partial to a particular gender. Both men and women alike need to be free from emotional demons that can hinder their walk with God.

The outward manifestations of deliverance are not always the same. Sometimes people mistakenly believe that if you're not falling out on the floor and spitting up, then you're not genuinely being delivered. They believe that if you are not literally running around the church, you are not delivered. You must understand that there are times when people did not even pray that earnestly for deliverance, yet were still delivered and set free by the power of God because the right people were praying with them, rebuking the devil out of them.

I believe it is important that deliverance be a continual process lest we find ourselves drawn back into those self-defeating sins, bad habits and attitudes that had us bound. Freedom is attained not by one single act of receiving God's Word but rather by growing in the Word of God, by growing in prayer and building up our devotional lives before God on a daily basis.

Don't allow anyone to convince you that deliverance is always instantaneous. Sometimes deliverance comes in different forms. The person who takes three days to get delivered is just as delivered as the person who took three hours to get delivered. I've seen people get delivered from a long-standing drug addiction in one hour. Just because they received a quick deliverance does not mean that they are going to walk in victory on that account alone.

That is why deliverance should be a part of our daily thought process. We must present ourselves before God daily. We must crucify the affections and the lusts of our flesh daily so that we can walk in deliverance. You might ask, "Could deliverance be total?" And, "Can it be permanent?" Yes, it can be permanent as long as you work at it. And it can be complete and total as long as you always remember what you had to go through to receive it, and even more what Christ had to go through for you to receive it.

Remember that there is no sin too great that God cannot totally deliver a person from. Don't allow the devil to fool you. Please don't allow the devil to discourage you. Just because you're tempted in an area does not mean that you are not delivered. I've heard people say that it is impossible to reform a drug addict. Nothing could be further from the truth. As soon as a drug addict is set free by the power of God, he is no longer bound by the power of drugs, *if* the *root* of the problem is dealt with.

A recovering drug addict or substance abuser can complete a whole lot of programs, receive their certificates and graduate with cap and gown. However, if they are not set free based on faith in God and His power to prohibit demon spirits from returning into their lives, it will be easier for them to continue to use drugs. Faith is the key to deliverance from any addiction. There is a group that I beg to differ with that says, "Once a drug addict, always a drug addict." I've witnessed God's supernatural power freeing men and women from drug addiction both within my ministry and in other churches and ministries.

There are no demon powers or addictions in this world stronger than the power of God. To believe there are is an insult to God. God is far greater than those powers. In the era that we live, many people have believed that homosexuality is a normal behavior and should be viewed the same way as heterosexual behavior. This is not true. I have seen men and women set free by the power of God from homosexuality and lesbianism. They tell their own testimonies of having been deceived by the devil and secular society into believing that their lifestyles were not unholy. When you are delivered, you are no longer in an agreement with your former licentious behavior. You've been set free!

If you are struggling with an area of addiction, I want you to pray this prayer out loud right now.

> *Lord, help me to hate the sins You hate and to love the things You love. Lord, help me to embrace those situations and attitudes that will only improve my quality of life. Lord, help me to embrace those habits that will enhance my spiritual well-being. Lord, help me to embrace, read and study those scriptures that will push me closer toward my destiny and purpose in this life. And also, Lord, help me to understand that I cannot do anything without You, but that through Christ I can do all things. In Jesus' Name, amen.*

Pray this prayer of deliverance over your life every day. When you begin to hate the sins that God hates and love the things that God loves, you will experience a whole new level of spiritual maturity and a higher level of freedom. If the truth was told and the devil had his way, none of us would be victorious in any area of our lives. We all would suffer from addictive behaviors and continue to be slaves to sin. That is why I am a firm believer that no one should be counted out. Everyone deserves a chance to be free.

Part One

The Devil Wanted Me to Kill My Kids

The Story of the Late Evangelist Alma Dickerson
(1929 – 1978)

❦

You will keep in perfect peace him whose mind is steadfast, because he trusts in you (Isaiah 26:3).

As Mommy bent over the kitchen sink, the devil gradually slipped deranged thoughts into her mind. "Go ahead and drown them," he told her as she washed the dirt off me and my siblings' faces. "You know you want to kill them." Those crazed voices parked themselves inside her head as the pain of rejection gradually overpowered her. By that time, most of her previous lovers had deserted her. Her family had left her to fend for herself. Day and night the voices kept her company in her "low-rent" apartment when her former lovers did not.

3

The voices delivered the same unrelenting messages. "Kill your six youngest children and yourself." She thought of acting on those homicidal and suicidal impulses, but something stopped her. The sounds became increasingly persistent on the day that she drove across the Tobin Bridge in Boston. The voices told her to throw her children over the rail into the Boston Harbor. As they looked over the water, the voices grew emphatically. "Throw the kids in the water. Kill the kids!" the devil shouted. "Jump in after them and DIE. Give your life up."

There was no turning off the voices, even as she tried to quiet the thoughts from her mind. Mom had worked part-time cleaning the floors of wealthy people's homes and as a stock clerk in local department stores. When the voices took over, it impaired her ability to work. To pacify herself, she would often walk aimlessly through the housing projects, trying to figure out honest ways to put food on the table for her six children.

The devil unremittingly badgered her, making false claims to relieve her from all her suffering. "Kill all six of the children. Kill yourself," he persisted. No matter what she tried to do, it seemed as if she couldn't break free. Rhetorical questions scurried through her clouded mind. "What kind of a man would want a single mother of eight children, especially if he had to feed the youngest six kids living with her?"

The best earplugs couldn't stop the demented voices from speaking to her inside of her head. She became increasingly deranged and paranoid. Strange people were planning to launch an attack against her, she thought. Killing her children seemed to be her best option to counteract the assault. The devil had complete control of all her rational thoughts. Her paranoid mind arduously labored overtime, as she relived memories of her troubled past.

Alma Rucker, the innocent attractive young girl from Selma, Alabama, gave her heart to a glib-talking man who was more than twice her age. He enticed her into living with him temporarily, just long enough to get her pregnant. There was just enough room in her momma's house for her, not a newborn baby. When her mother found out that Alma was pregnant she was upset but decided to take in the baby boy. However, Grandma Rucker showed my mom the door and she wound up on the streets again, kicked out of the house. Shamed and ostracized, she roamed from house to house at the tender age of 13, looking for love in all the wrong places, trying to find a sense of belonging.

When one family member suggested that she pack up to go and live with her relatives in Boston, she took the money and headed north. Nothing could have prepared young Alma's eyes for the slick streets of Boston, totally opposite to Selma culture. She became exposed to hard-core city life where she witnessed prostitution, muggings, increased drug and alcohol abuse and occasional stabbings in broad open daylight in her own environment.

She watched other people muddle through the very last days of the Great Depression by sniffing drugs and drinking cough medicine to relieve them from their present darkness. Alma had a newborn baby and was determined to survive, even if she had to do it alone. The young, voluptuous, big-boned, teenage beauty from Selma had bought into the dreams that many southern girls hear about better opportunities up in the north. She quickly learned that Boston was not all that she dreamed it would be and its streets were not streets of gold, especially for a young, black, single mother.

Although she looked seemingly everywhere and would do most anything to support her baby, nobody offered her a job. Desperate, she found herself in sleazy nightclubs where she was forced to lash out at life's unexpected blows with her knuckles and fists. In these clubs, brown-skinned men often approached her with promises of a better life, fine jewels and the other fineries of life. They never came through. Other women in the bars couldn't help but be jealous that this new-comer was getting all this attention.

One woman underestimated young Alma's quick wit and southern charm when she talked up a fight. Alma met the challenge but found out years later that acting out her temper stole away parts of her soul. "Well, if I fight you, it really would-n't be a fight. Why don't you get your two friends from over there, and let's really make it a fight," Alma boasted. Feeling isolated from her family and rejected by so many former lovers, she released the rage she was suppressing within her-self with every knuckle punch she delivered.

Although she had a tough outer layer, inside she was still a naïve southern girl who attracted fast guys. Her naïveté led her right into the arms of a U.S. Navy sailor, Dillie F. Dugan Jr. She thought she had found the love of her life, but that relationship proved to be wrong. The rocky relationship ended in divorce after much drama and emotional strain. As the 1960s ushered in Black Power and self-discovery, she felt grossly rejected and heartbroken. Disappointed repeat-edly by men and family members who refused to return the love that she so kindly offered, Mom had to battle off and on

6

with depression. She soon found out that social activities could not placate her pain.

Over several years the trauma of repeated rejections and being a single mother of eight children took its toll on her emotions and her psychological stability. Mom reached her breaking point and finally had a nervous breakdown. That is when the voices began speaking to her. Alma was already vulnerable, and the voices quickly convinced her that her life was not worth living. She readily agreed. She sought help from believers. However, she never followed the biblical plan of action that they prescribed for her. The devil had a stronghold on her and was not going to let her go—not without a fight.

As a result of her nervous breakdown, she was committed to a mental institution in Boston. Her family all agreed that this would be the best thing for her considering her fragile condition. The children had to fend for themselves until some relatives took them in. Fortunately, some of her sisters and her brothers cared for us until foster homes became available. Thank God, my dad, William E. Dickerson Sr., took me to his mother's after Grandma made it clear to him, "I want William Jr. to come and live with me because he is just a baby."

While institutionalized my mother discovered a new comfort. Her mind broke through the haze of pills and sedatives when she cried out to God. She believed that God would deliver her from tormenting voices, suicidal spirits, and demons of abuse and neglect that molested her. She prayed the simplest prayer with high anticipation and childlike sincerity. *"God, if You deliver me from this mental institution and give me back my right mind and bring me back to my children, then I will serve You until the day I die."*

Although the vast majority of people institutionalized never experience freedom from their demons, God answered her prayers in the most miraculous sense. He restored her to her right mind and reunited her with her children. Keeping her promise to Him, she began to learn how to trust God and depend on His Word. She counted those experiences as valuable fundamental lessons about what God was capable of doing in the life of a surrendered soul. She began to grow in the Word of God, studying the Bible every chance that she got and praying several time each day.

Evangelist Alma began to share her powerful story of deliverance with other people. Each time she told her story, she received new strength and confidence. Just to think, God delivered her from the tormenting spirits that tried to get her to kill herself and her children. That thought alone is absolutely amazing. Her new life in Christ was so much greater than her old life in sin that she became totally dedicated to the Lord, almost to the point of obsession. For the rest of her life, she honored her word by evangelizing and becoming a promulgator of the deliverance message.

My mother married my father, William E. Dickerson Sr., and he reared my other siblings as if they were his own. My mom continued to rear all her children in church and a loving home atmosphere. Although some of my siblings strayed away from the faith, her example of righteousness and Christian virtue remains one that I have not seen anything like since. I thank God for my mother. Throughout my lifetime, I have never met anyone with her unwavering love for people. Realizing that she herself was a product of God's delivering power, she always looked on others through God's eyes, never judging them or giving up on anyone.

8

I remember watching in amazement as she would literally feed hungry people on the streets in the ghetto and then preach the Word of the Lord to them. She fed drug addicts, prostitutes and homeless people. Her ministry was a family affair. In fact, I learned how to operate street ministry from watching my mother. Whenever God led my mother to do so, we would load up the car with sandwiches and other goodies and pass them out to people downtown, right near the Boston Commons and at the Northampton bus station.

Sister Alma continually stood on the Word of God that says "whom the Son has made free is free indeed" (see John 8:36). God set her free. He gave her the power to heal, to deliver and to set people free from the bondage of addiction. What God did for my mother is possible for anyone who suffers from her same condition. Many people may consider it impossible or may even try to deny the authenticity of such deliverance. However, I am living proof and a product of her deliverance. So I know firsthand that it is real.

If you have ever dealt with suicidal spirits, abusive relationships or the pain of rejection from loved ones, God can deliver you. Perhaps you have encountered a nervous breakdown and cannot see yourself living past that moment. God will restore you to your full strength and full mental faculty, and He will anoint you and help you to overcome every dilemma from your past. God delivered the late Reverend Alma Dickerson, affectionately known as "Sister." The same possibility is available to you.

So if the Son sets you free, you will be free indeed (John 8:36).

Mitigating the Hardest Heart

The Story of Dillie Dugan III, aka Deke
(1951 – 1986)

❧❦❧

He lifted me out of the slimy pit, out of the mud and mire; he set my feet on a rock and gave me a firm place to stand (Psalm 40:2).

When my older brother Dillie (Deke) was at his worst, he often put extreme fear in the hearts of some of the vilest people on the streets. In the wee hours of the night running into the early morning, when junkies and dope dealers were nodding out, Dillie kicked down doors in back allies and crowded drug dens. "Police! Give it up!" he'd run through the doors shouting. Most times, Dillie didn't even wear a face mask when he ordered drug dealers to empty their pockets. They threw their tiny bags of heroin and crumpled bills to the floor.

11

He picked up the stash and boldly walked out of these drug dens. He played the big bad rogue pretty well. The gangsters couldn't believe that Dillie, once a big-time dealer in Boston, had become so desperate for money and drugs. Little did they know: the big muscular thug had a terrible drug habit that he could not kick. As the word leaked out that Dillie was crazy for the "stuff," the small-time dealers who earned a living slinging dope would break a little off their packages for Dillie so he wouldn't take all they had.

In short Dillie was totally crazed. He would stick up, beat up or whip up on any small-time dealer, prostitute or even hustler who didn't play the game by his rules. Not caring for his own life, he was totally blasé about whether he would get caught or not. Prison for a junkie like Dillie was more like a recess and a break from the fast life than doing time. In some ways, when he was in prison he felt like he had some time to recuperate from the mean streets and fast life in which he lived.

Prison was the place to go especially in the winter, when being dope sick just wasn't any fun. Jail was the junkie's vacation plan and HMO plan. He was as slick as a fox knowing never to do anything too appalling since he did not want to do long time. But if he needed a break from chasing dope, he'd usually take a break when it was real cold or when he got tired of running from the law.

Dillie got caught up in the dope scene early on. When other young black boys were throwing their fists up in the air shouting "Black Power," following the lead of Huey Newton and the Black Panthers in the 1960s, and when other young black men were going to jail for just causes like social activism and civil rights, Dillie was smoking weed with his

12

friends. When he turned 16, instead of graduating from high school, he graduated to snorting heroin and was instantly hooked.

Dillie, who went by the street name Deke, always lived life in the fast lane. Dillie named himself Deke and the name was adopted by family members and friends. Later, because Deke was so impressed with the styles and images of the street hustlers of Detroit, Michigan, he added to his street name. He coined the phrase "Sweet Deke from Detroit," although he never lived in that city. School became secondary to his newfound friends, the ones who schooled him while luring him into their crime-filled world. The older kids in the projects where he lived taught him how to make money. It wasn't long before he had his very own job, selling drugs and running his own crew.

In the early years, Deke hid his drugs at our mother's house. He was trying to get ahead of the game, but he really didn't trust many people with his stash. One time our mother found tiny sandwich bags filled with white powder. They were hidden behind a chest in the attic of the place in the Dorchester section of Boston where we lived at the time. She balled up the dope in her fists and marched militantly downstairs to the bathroom. She gleefully threw the bags into the toilet bowl, one by one. In one sense it appeared that she was doing this to save her son's life and secure his not-so-promising future, if that was even possible.

As she flushed each bag down the toilet, her mind raced. She did not fully understand at that point that whoever gave this junk to her son Deke would inevitably come to her house looking for him. The drug supplier might even try to kill her son. That reality dawned on her as she watched each bag circle round and round the toilet bowl as the white stuff went down the drain.

Little did she know that her son was the drug dealer. Like a courier carrying a first-class parcel, Deke made his runs from Boston to New York and back to Boston to pick up his supply. He had a few of the neighborhood teenagers and some older men selling the drugs for him. By this time street life had so consumed him that he had become a dreadful man, one of the most feared men in Boston.

Added to his drug dealing, Deke also started working as a pimp to support his own drug habit. He sweet-talked a few girls to prostitute on the street for him to keep his cash flow steadily coming in. He moved from one house to the next house just to avoid the police. Never stationary, he lived his life always on the run, always on the go. A very sharp dresser, Deke was very clean, neat and always well groomed, which was one of his selling points with the women he pursued.

Although he was real popular with the ladies, he brought mostly negative attention to himself when he hung around other drug dealers and pimps. He forever lived knowing that the police would at some point catch up with him and send him to jail for committing one or more criminal acts. There were times when he went to prison and it was a blessing in disguise.

One time when he was in prison, there was a hit out on his life. Because he was in prison he was protected from the threat of assassination. However, the prisoners who were involved from the inside beat him so badly that our mother didn't even recognize him when she visited him after he was hospitalized due to this vicious attack. By the grace of God he survived that ordeal.

One other time the police shot at him as he was running away into an open field. I was only about 11 years old when I nervously watched the police empty their guns in an attempt to wound or kill my brother. My mom prayed while a few of my siblings and I cried. But again by the grace of God he managed to escape death. Every time the police caught up with him, they'd put him in jail. Like clockwork Dillie got out and was back at the street game again. Death always seemed to want to claim my brother. When one attempt at taking his life failed, another one was always waiting.

One day a man walked up to Dillie and shot him about six times at point-blank range. Dillie put up his hands and actually caught two bullets that could have fatally wounded him. In fact, for the rest of his life he had a bullet permanently lodged near his heart. The doctors did not want to remove it because he could have died on the operating table. To the average onlooker, possibly even a physician, it would appear as if Dillie was gone for good. Rumors had even started to circulate on the streets that he had died in a brutal shooting. Amazingly God spared his life again. Once he recovered and got back out on the streets, people started calling him "Nine-Lives," thinking that he was indestructible.

Dillie went through so many trials, so many ups and downs, trying to maintain his life as a drug dealer, a pimp and an addict. The juggling became a bit strenuous, as he was getting older. Eventually Dillie married a woman who did not cause him to settle down as many wives do, but rather to fire up and take the whole game to an entirely different level. His wife was downright ruthless. She became his partner in crime. Together they mastered con games.

When she went into one room to turn a trick, she captured the unassuming stranger's attention long enough for Dillie to ransack the guy's pockets for money. They were the dynamic duo scamming people wherever they went. To watch them in action, any drama major would swear that they rehearsed their lines. They didn't even have to rehearse the con games; no dress rehearsal needed. They felt the vibe so strong and that vibe meant going for the greenbacks in some total stranger's pockets.

At one point in his life, Deke used to carry two guns: one on his hip so the mark would see it, and the other one hidden inside his jacket or coat. His wife, equally as notorious as he was, carried a small hatchet in her evening bag. She was a tough, tough woman, tougher than most men. In the midst of all that they were involved in, turning toward God never entered either of their minds.

While they were steeped in their sins, at the height of their disreputable behavior, God was calling them. He was clearing an open road for their deliverance. When Deke's drug habit became sorely out of control, our mother held small prayer meetings. She'd invite Deke into the circle to pray for deliverance. Deke would bow his head, say the sinner's prayer and nod off into a heroin ecstasy. That did not matter to my mom because she stayed steadfast in prayer. She prophesied over his life and asked God to deliver him and to bring him out. No matter how bad the circumstances appeared, she lived with the unfailing conviction that one day her son would be free.

More than 19 years had passed since his first involvement with drugs and now Deke was too strung out to operate his drug empire any longer. That game was over. Not only was he disappointed by the fact that he could no longer play the game anymore, he was also devastated by the most shocking news of his life. On a particular visit to the doctors, after a series of tests, the doctors informed him that he had incurable cancer of the throat. The cancer caused a large puss-filled lump to protrude from his neck.

That was in 1986, the most difficult year in his life. He was deathly ill, and the people he wanted to hang with him didn't want to be around him anymore. All of his so-called street buddies deserted him. This was the first time in his life when God actually had his undivided attention. He withered down from a strapping 235 pounds to about 145 pounds. All of the girls he used to date or pimp on the streets abandoned him too. All the "Slick Willies" who used to beg to be in his company and used to dream of one day being a big-time street hustler like him now saw Deke as a sick drug addict with throat cancer.

Deke suffered greatly during that awful fight against that affliction. In his suffering, he was able to recognize that he belonged to a praying family, a most valuable legacy. We stayed faithfully by his side praying for him and interceding on his behalf. Six weeks before he died, Deke found comfort and strength listening to Rev. R.W. Schambach and Evangelist Jimmy Swaggart and other preachers on the radio. For the first time in his life he was starving for the Gospel and seized every opportunity to hear it whenever he could.

My brother Lawrence and I regularly ministered to Dillie. We visited Dillie and saw him praying and reading his Bible. Dillie succumbed to throat cancer, but not before he accepted Jesus Christ as Lord and Savior nearly six weeks before he died. The Bible says in 2 Corinthians 5:8, *"We are confident, I say, and would prefer to be away from the body and at home with the Lord."* God can soften the heart of the hardest sinner and cause him or her to become as meek and humble as a lamb.

Hard street life has the power to draw people under with its hypnotic control and addictive snare. It is filled with traumatic experiences, drugs, prostitution, conning, stealing, cheating and illicit sexuality. Its appearance may at first glance look inviting, but it is no more than a smokescreen with death lurking behind its curtains. God delivered my brother from the power of drug addiction, illicit drug selling, pimping and more. Dillie's body decayed from cancer, but his spirit, which is eternal, is with God.

Although God is not the author of sickness and disease, sickness came upon my brother to give him a much-needed wake-up call, causing him to commit his life to Christ. Dillie cried out to God and He delivered him. God is no respecter of persons. However, He is a respecter of faith. And if you have the faith to believe that He will deliver you from your burning hell, He will.

For, "Everyone who calls on the name of the Lord will be saved" (Romans 10:13).

The Sins of the Family: The Story of My Birth

Testimony of Shawn L. Watson

❧❦❧

Then God said to Abraham, "As for you, you must keep my covenant, you and your descendants after you for the generations to come" (Genesis 17:9).

Filled with a myriad of mixed emotions—grief, anger, fear and blind optimism—my mother held me in her arms gazing into my infant eyes shortly after giving birth to me. Though I was the product of rape, she still felt an inescapable maternal attachment to her newborn baby. My mother named me Shawn. She desperately needed somebody to love and it would be me, her only child. Even before I breathed my very first breath, my life was destined for unusual drama.

My father, the man who raped my mother, had been dating my aunt, my mother's older sister. My aunt was the mother of his firstborn child and despite the many telltale signs of his profligate behavior, she still thought that he would qualify as a good husband for her. Confused and trapped, he was in a huge quandary as he lusted after both sisters, sincerely believing that he loved them both. To deal with his insatiable cravings toward my mom, the more vulnerable of the two sisters, he raped her.

Some people in my family labeled me an "accident." Others viewed my birth as another grief-stricken episode in the story of my mother's life. Most saw it as a shameful and disgraceful stain on the family's reputation. Although my aunt strongly urged her to get an abortion, my grandmother continued to stick by her and encouraged her to keep the child and preserve a human life. My mother heeded grandmother's words and I was born on February 14, 1969.

At first my mother considered my birth as a new beginning for her, sort of a new start in life. However, being a single mother under these abnormal circumstances would prove to be far too much for her to handle. After I was born my aunt became increasingly angry. She was mad because she saw my birth as a potential threat to her nuptial plans. My aunt was still foolishly determined to marry the man, despite the crime of rape, the disgrace that he brought on our family, and the potential of separating two sisters.

She was so desperate and strong-minded that she threatened him that if he didn't go through with the wedding, she would personally report the rape to the police. As for my mother, from the very beginning she got off to a very dim start. She was born prematurely to a mother who struggled with alcoholism. My mom was diagnosed at birth with a bad heart condition, somewhat of a heart murmur. Added to her tall list of juvenile maladies were epilepsy, bad vision and an apparent psychological instability.

Sickness and not having the proper support from her mother were reason enough to develop a serious complex, but even her maternal side of the family continually took advantage of her all her life. With all of her pressures escalating each day and not having a proper outlet to release her frustrations, she began using alcohol as her sweet comfort. It was something to take her away from the vicissitudes of life, even if just for a moment. Although she began using this substance as a sort of temporary fix for her present problems, this curse of alcoholism would unfortunately follow her throughout her life.

As with any substance abuse problem, it only gets worse as time goes on if not dealt with early on. It was no different with my mother. Her condition got so bad and she became so careless with caring for me that my grandmother decided to take me. Then my mother could freely run the streets without having to deal with the guilt of blatant child neglect. Grandma did the best she could in rearing me for the first eight years of my life, given her limited resources. However, that would only be a short-lived span.

When I was eight, my grandmother's health began to get really bad. She started getting awfully sick and eventually had to be admitted into a nursing home for specialized treatment. Sadly, my grandmother, my first genuine love connection, died in that convalescent home, forcing me to find someone to live with all over again. There weren't a whole lot of choices for me, so I ended up living with my aunt, uncle and four cousins in the Roxbury section of Boston.

It was crazy living there. I mean, I was always exposed to and encircled by people living in the most poverty-stricken conditions. And, boy, was I exposed to that poverty in a very singular way. Although I lived with my relatives, I was really not treated as one of the bunch. They treated me more like an outsider rather than as a part of a family to which I legitimately belonged. I never got seconds when we ate. There was no extra cornbread for me at the dinner table. My cousins' appetites were always first priority. I would never even dream that I would be given preferential treatment when it came to them.

I used to wear my cousins' hand-me-downs because my aunt and uncle didn't believe that I was worth spending the money for new clothes. Secondhand, second place and second fiddle all became too familiar expressions of life. I adopted a tolerance for having only second or third best of everything, never first quality apparel or food. As a child, even though you know deep within that something is just not right about partiality and injustice, you really can't say anything about it. So that you would continue to have a place to stay, you just had to shut up concerning issues that were dear to you.

I didn't have the "crème de la crème," the best things in life, but overall I was still very grateful. I was grateful to have a place to live. And life with my aunt, uncle and cousins was especially exciting and at times extremely dangerous. My aunt, who was the disciplinarian in the family, was also a homemaker who very seriously considered raising her five boys in their house. I can clearly remember how she would whip us when we did something wrong.

In her mind she used to whip us to keep us in line. She used what I would call "creative whipping strategies." She

22

would use almost anything that she could find to whip us: brooms, ironing cords, pots, switches and anything else within her reach. My uncle was a short, muscular and fairly quiet man. He very seldom yelled at us. The very few times that he would, he ripped off his wide-leather belt and gave us a whooping we didn't soon forget.

My aunt and uncle unofficially adopted me as their son. Yet, I still yearned to know who my real father was. From time to time during my childhood, I broached the subject with my aunts and my mother. I wanted some information, any information that would lead me to my real father. They'd pacify me with tall tales in an effort to keep me quiet and to extinguish my curiosity. "What about the war?" I'd ask. "When was my father coming back from the war?" I thought this had to be the longest war of all time, longer than World War I, World War II and Vietnam combined.

My aunt knew that my inquisitiveness could not be easily satisfied so she decided to end all discussions on the matter by informing me that my father had died during combat. Although her story seemed to bring a bit of closure to my life, a whole new avenue of discovery started to rise when I began noticing some very obvious finds. During my teenage years I would check out my facial features in the mirror, something that many teenagers commonly do in their pastimes.

Strangely, I would notice that I looked more like my uncle than his own sons did. One day for some reason, maybe because he knew that my search would never end, he decided to confess the truth—that he was my real father. All these years I sincerely wanted to know the truth about my beginnings, I longed to know who my real father was.

Now I actually heard the truth for the first time, and the truth was a bit weird to accept at first.

He told me that he was genuinely sorry for not telling me this sooner. The man I was living with, my aunt's husband, my uncle, was also my father. I was so confused but I felt obligated to forgive him. He had always been there for me. After living with him for 15 years, I had learned to love and respect him. One thing he never confessed to me, though, was that he had raped my mother, his wife's sister. I guess some things you just are not supposed to tell.

Feelings of abandonment began to grow in my emotions. I started to feel overwhelmed by the pain of massive rejection. Eventually drugs and alcohol became my comforting outlet. In my family, substance abuse and drug addiction were quite common. I would join the generations of people in my family who regularly abused drugs and alcohol to hide a sense of worthlessness. Just thinking about all of this made me begin to hate others and myself.

I heard voices inside me sounding much like a commanding sergeant giving high orders to use strong illegal narcotics. These drugs would dull my inner pain and slowly numb my feelings from the inside out. My drug problems became progressively worse. I went from smoking marijuana to cigarettes, then crack and cocaine. I used acid and drank alcohol from junior high school until I reached my twenties.

I totally ignored the fact that I had health problems. I had an enlarged heart and would often have seizures while I was in high school. Despite this I still used cocaine and alcohol almost every day. I really didn't care about living a "quality life." The doctor prescribed special medications to control

24

my seizures. I can remember several times that the seizures nearly killed me. God kept sparing my life from premature death and I really couldn't understand why.

Before I gave my life to God, I lived comfortably with the devil within me. I transformed into a selfish thief, one who would blame the whole world, including God, for all my misfortunes in life. Even though I went to church as a boy, I did not believe that Jesus was the answer despite what all those preachers said. Personally I believed that everything they were saying was a bunch of hype. I had seen too many church people getting high and scheming just like me. I knew that they could not be any better than I was if they were bound like me.

The evil voices continued to speak to me. I got high with anybody who wanted to share the joint or give me a hit from the pipe. One night I can remember, some friends and I were getting high. While we were fired up, I mean totally high, we began to talk about Jesus. Folks who get high have some very interesting outlooks about the Divine. Everyone in the room had something to say. Although they didn't have a relationship with God, my friends believed that He existed. They believed that there was a God somewhere out there.

I was the one who stood up in defiance and protested. "There is no God," I insisted. Anger rose up within me and like an educated atheist I told the group that I could prove to them that the Bible was a great big lie and greatly contradicted itself in many places. I went into the living room and opened up my grandmother's Bible and began to read it aloud, mimicking the Scriptures. I didn't really know what I was talking about; I just wanted to defy whatever I could.

The real truth was that I was mad at God. That is why I wanted to discredit Him.

I felt that if there was a God, then why would He allow my life to be such a big mess? Why wouldn't He care about me? Even though my friends were as high as kites, they still had a learned fear of God. They all left me there by myself. They did not want to play with God and they really did not think that my mimicking and mockery of God was funny. They believed that I had gone too far in my demonstration. Before I knew it I was left high and dry, holding the Bible in my hand, while they exited through the door.

The very next night I was smoking a joint alone, and I picked up the Bible again and began to read it. From that night I found myself reading the Bible every time I got high. My friends thought I was crazy. They wanted no part of this madness. My relatives talked about how the family's drug head was now reading the Bible. I kept offering God a challenge. "If You are real, show me and help me,"' I told God. "Why would You create me and not reveal Yourself to me?"

About one week from that time, I was walking a downtown street and totally unbeknownst to me God met my challenge. A Christian brother named Wallace Brown invited me to his church, Greater Love Tabernacle. I quickly gave my telephone number to him just to get him out of my face. That was a bad mistake, or so I thought. He called me repeatedly until I finally broke and went with him to a service. So I went with him just so he would stop calling. It was sort of my punishment being paid in full for giving him my number in the first place.

As soon as I walked into the sanctuary, I immediately felt something very different, something very strange. I sensed a powerful spirit within me. A part of me felt so good, so right, but I was very afraid and I really did not know why. The words of the pastor, Pastor William Dickerson, were like sharp blows attacking something inside me. It seemed as if somebody gave him some inside information on my life. The message seemed so personally tailored for me. Because of that, I felt restless and began tossing and turning in my seat like a four-year-old child would during a long and boring worship service.

While I listened to the pastor as he spoke, I felt demonic spirits rising up in me and demanding that I get out of there. This was the same voice that I had obeyed since childhood. This was the same voice that encouraged me to smoke my first joint, drink my first beer, smoke my first cigarette, tell my first lie, steal my first candy bar, sniff my first $20 bag of cocaine and smoke my first piece of crack. I was very certain whose voice was speaking to me, as I had come to know this voice as clearly as I could recognize my aunt's voice or my cousins'. It was really that clear.

For the first time in my life I exercised the audacity to actually defy the voices. I kept my ears fixed on every word that the pastor was speaking. Deep down I wanted to hear what he had to say and I wasn't going to miss it. In some ways it seemed like my ability to hear this man's message was my only way out of my madness. I successfully warded off the voices, but then my body started to shake right during the message.

The voices inside me were obviously angered by the fact that I was intentionally ignoring them, so they became indignant and yelled out, "Enough of this! You have to go!" The demonic spirits exposed themselves before the congregation

27

and everyone took notice. The spirits started to take control of my arms, my legs and my voice. The voices kept talking and I became an obvious disturbance to the service that was going on.

The evil spirits started talking real crazy, urging me to run out of the sanctuary and into traffic in the street. Of course the spirits knew that they could find another body to torment. But they would not leave my body until they accomplished their goal. And their main mission was to deliver my soul to the devil before I could find salvation in Jesus Christ.

I had become totally out of control during the service, absolutely belligerent in my actions. Several of the brothers in the church tackled me with the force of NFL linebackers. The unclean spirits living inside of me used my small body at that time to wrestle with them right on the sanctuary floor. The pastor watched this battle between the church brothers and the demonic spirits inside me. It got worse, so the pastor sent the children out of the sanctuary.

I starting cursing up a storm, "Get the —— off of me." The devil was using me to overthrow these men of God. He was angry that these people were trying to stop his progress of destroying my life. That did not intimidate the believers at Greater Love one bit. They remained steadfast. They continued to call on the Name of Jesus and spoke the Word of God with authority. Because of this the evil spirits fled from my body.

Some of the spirits left my body immediately. They left so swiftly that it caused parts of my body to begin sweating profusely. My legs went completely limp. I could barely stand up. Some of the demon spirits tried fighting me physically, making my body jerk as if I were having a horrible seizure. Hours went by and there was still work to do; there were more demons that needed to be cast out of me.

I remember Pastor Dickerson placing the palm of his hand on my forehead as God used him to cast out the remaining spirits. Angered by the power of Christ working in him, the spirits tried one last attempt to kill me. The demon blurted out, "You cannot have him! He is mine!" The spirit spoke and then thrust my head right through a sheet-rock wall. Pastor instructed the brothers standing by to take my head out of the wall. With power and authority he told the devil that he no longer had power over me. I remember him saying these words with power and authority, "Loose him in the Name of Jesus Christ."

With that, I sat up, yet I was obviously physically beaten. I literally had bruises on the back of my head and my face. In spite of what I looked like physically, I was so happy to be free of many of the evil spirits that had controlled me all my life. For the first time in my life I was truly free from all the pain of my past and the shame of my birth. My own "prison complex" no longer incarcerated me in my mind. It felt like experiencing the fresh air an inmate inhales after being locked in isolation for decades.

I believe more than anything that God sovereignly used the pastor and his staff by His anointing to help set me free from those demons. There is not one day that I am not thankful to God for my pastor. He taught me by example and mentored me about the miraculous love of God, something that I will never forget. Both he and his wife showed me God's love, not just in words but also in deeds and practice. They never stopped praying for me.

Now after 14 years, I remain free from the demon spirits and strongholds that bound me. I now serve as a Prophetic Minister in our church. I've been married for ten years and have three lovely children. The devil had plans for my life that are far different than how I am living right now. This I know for sure: God broke the generational curses on my life, which would have continued through my posterity had I not been delivered.

And he passed in front of Moses, proclaiming, "The LORD, the LORD, the compassionate and gracious God, slow to anger, abounding in love and faithfulness, maintaining love to thousands, and forgiving wickedness, rebellion and sin. Yet he does not leave the guilty unpunished; he punishes the children and their children for the sin of the fathers to the third and fourth generation" (Exodus 34:6-7).

Rescued from Spousal Abuse

The Story of Minister Barbara A. Dulin

❧❧❧

Husbands, love your wives and do not be harsh with them (Colossians 3:19).

M y mother had always taught me to be a good girl. Whenever she needed help with my seven younger brothers and sisters, I would cook their meals and help them with their homework. I was a very happy child with a winning smile. I was always filled with joy and laughter. My grandmother, whom we affectionately called Big Mom, also played an important role in my developmental years and added to my cheerfulness.

People would always notice how I loved to cling to Big Mom. After all, Big Mom was the one who taught me the first Bible verse that I committed to memory. She often said, *"I will never leave you nor forsake you"* (Hebrews 13:5 NKJV). She forever reminded me as a little girl, "Jesus is our provider, honey." Little did I know then how much I would need to cling to those words for my very survival in the years to come.

When I wasn't sitting up under Big Mom, I played school with my brothers and sisters. At night, after I helped put them to bed, I used to struggle trying to complete my own homework assignments. I never sought out help because so many others looked up to me as their role model and depended on me as the family's helper. I always had to be strong for everyone else even when no one was strong for me. That was tough. But I seemed to manage it.

My life would get even more difficult when my mother decided that we would move to Boston. Boston wasn't the real issue; Big Mom was. Big Mom was not going to make the move with us, which meant that I would no longer have her to cling to. Her absence caused me to start making decisions on my own, ones that I should have made and decisions that should probably have been made with the help of wise adults.

One decision that I made without being properly guided was to drop out of school after my sophomore year. Ashamed by my hasty choice, I lied for years about why I dropped out. I told everyone that I'd quit school to go to work. "Momma needs help financially to make ends meet, so I need to help my family out." The real reason that I dropped out of school is that I felt inadequate. I had little confidence that I would be able to be passed onto the next grade. Without ever really trying, I had disqualified myself. The days ahead would serve as a living witness of just how uninformed a decision that actually was.

As with most dropouts, it didn't take long for me to get into trouble. I was just eighteen years old when my boyfriend, a high school graduate and an ex-convict, got me pregnant. He did not love me and I really did not know what love was all about. Despite that, we decided to get married anyway. For me it was about pride, about hiding my shame, about giving my child his father's name, and about having a family. Those were my objectives, and no one could change my mind.

I ignored all the people who continued to tell me that I could do better and that I would eventually ruin my life. No matter what they said, nothing would stop me from getting married. Most newlyweds look forward to a honeymoon. My honeymoon was over before the marriage even got started. From the start, we argued over just about everything. My husband would tell me that he could not find work, but he always managed to stay out late night with his friends.

I took a job that paid minimum wages just to keep food on the table. By the time my son was born, I was mentally, physically and emotionally exhausted. I felt trapped in a dead-end relationship that seemed quite hopeless, yet I did not know what to do or where to go. My husband, on the other hand, ended his search for honest work. He was convinced that he would make a far more lucrative income being a pimp. He wasted no time as he began honing his new professional skills by charming women and picking out possible Johns from bar stools where he hung out at each night.

Every night he was gone and I was left alone with the sole responsibility of rearing our child. Each night I put our baby to bed and then go to sleep alone. When I questioned my husband about where he spent his time, he would curse me out. His whole demeanor toward women changed almost overnight. He would use the most profane language, calling me every four-letter word in the book. My husband never distinguished me from the whores that he used to prostitute; he would talk to me the same way that he did to them.

His late-night stays gradually turned into not coming home for several nights at a time. While he was away from home I began to feel sorry for myself, but, I also began to evaluate my life. The compendium of my life—I quit school, left my loving family, and married a certified bum. The more I realized that truth the more depressed I became. But my depression and feeling sorry for myself did not seem to stop me from having a second child with this loser.

After our second child was born, I began to realize that I desperately needed a support system. I knew that I could not depend on my husband, so I felt that I had to do something that would free me from my present crisis. All I could think about was Big Mom and how she loved the Lord so much. I remember the peace that she owned just knowing that Jesus loved her. I thought if God worked for Big Mom, then possibly God would work things out in my life also.

I decided to join the local Pentecostal church, where I rededicated my life to the Lord Jesus Christ and was baptized in water. Trying to turn my ship totally around I also had my pastor dedicate both of my children to the Lord. Although I was making the right strides toward my spiritual freedom, behind the scenes the devil was setting a trap. My life immediately took a drastic turn for the worse. My husband, who was never really interested in my development one way or the other, refused to go to church with me and didn't want me to go either.

We fought every Sunday morning while I was preparing for church services. He opposed my choice, but I knew that my decision to follow Jesus was not up to him so I went anyway. Although I found a release in being in church I would sit in the back of the church, too afraid of the front row pews where I'd be closer to God, I thought. The pain of the whole situation and the hurt that I was feeling overwhelmed me. I was married to a man who was becoming a pimp.

My husband's mind became increasingly corrupted. He believed that a good pimp had to be true to his profession. And being true meant that he had to practice what he preached, starting at home. He actually wanted me to be his first girl on the stroll. Imagine that, he wanted his wife to become a whore. He told me that I could make more money working for him than if I held down a regular job. He added, "The kids need new clothes and I like to eat steaks."

I did not feel any draw toward his philosophical madness. If he was going to eat steaks and my kids would wear new clothes, it was going happen some other way. No matter how hard he tried to convince me, I resisted. Although I had made some mistakes along the way, up until this time in my life I had been a good girl and I wanted it to stay that way. So no matter how hard he tried, I refused, even if it meant that we had to fight. And we really fought.

He would hit me and I would try to hit him back, but he was so obviously bigger than I was that I was no match for him. He would beat me so mercilessly that I would be bruised all over. I used to wear big sunglasses and Jackie O style scarves just to hide the body bruises, my swollen eyes and my fat busted lips from my family and friends. I'd never invite my family over for dinner and I prayed that no one would ever pop in for a surprise visit.

It was the worst of times. My husband spent his evenings trying to force me to prostitute for him and it always ended with my getting severely beaten when I resisted. He forced me to wear ruby red lipstick, thick black eyeliner and fake eyelashes whenever the swelling went down. He then tried to make me wear these scanty short dresses with ridiculously high heels. As usual I refused and he just hit me harder with each refusal.

The man was crazy and I was sadly in his clutches although I wanted to be free. He punched me in my face, knocked me down, pushed me into the bedroom, and made me read chapters out loud from collections of books and dirty magazines on "the rules of the pimp game." Often times, he would literally tie my wrists to the bed and have abusive sexual intercourse with me against my will as he acted out his sick fantasies, playing the role of being a master pimp.

Whenever I called the police for help, they always let him go. Back then the police were partial toward the man's perspective. They never recorded the incidents from a battered wife's point of view. They listed each incident pretty much as a normal domestic problem, trivializing the magnitude of my dilemma. Right after the cops would leave, he would slap me down to the ground and say, "Now call your great white hope again. I'll kill you if you ever call them again."

Without even recuperating from the last incident, I found myself sitting on a brown wooden barstool, hearing my husband order me a rum and coke. On the way to the bar, I felt so worn out and fatigued from all of the quarreling I couldn't even fight back. He told me, "Tonight will be your first night to turn your first trick for me." I remember being so scared while I reluctantly put on my dress and makeup. All I could do was quietly pray for divine intervention. "Father, help me. Father, I need You."

Now, as I sat in the bar, I stared blankly as my husband eagerly looked around the room for my first sexual conquest, my first client. The room was dark and there were people on the dance floor seeming as if they were having a great time dancing. I noticed that there were a lot of African-American women wearing incredible wigs and dark shades as they danced with white men while the black men on barstools watched nearby.

They must be the pimps, I thought. In my whole life, I had never been exposed to or seen anything like this before. It was so strange, kind of like I was in a movie or something. After finishing my drink, my husband smiled at me and pointed out the stranger he had picked for me. "There is your trick," he said. I remember begging my husband not to make me go over there. I was so scared my knees buckled. My body started to slide out of the booth onto the floor.

Suddenly everything went totally black. To this day, that is all I can actually remember about that night after I fainted. When I came to my senses I found myself in a taxicab on my way home. I never really knew what happened that night. My husband later told me that when I started to stand up, I passed out cold on the floor. They brightened the lights as high as they could go, as people continually tried to wake me up.

My husband knew that he had to get me out of there quickly before anyone called an ambulance. He knew that the doctors would quickly notice that I had been abused. Looking back in retrospect, I believe that my fainting was a supernatural intervention by the Father who gave His angel charge over my life. It was God's way of releasing me from having to perform illicit acts and maintain the virtue that I wanted back so badly.

A few days later, I packed a change of clothing into two pillowcases and ran away from home with my children. I was so afraid that my husband would find us and kill us that I jumped every time I heard a loud sound outside. It was hard for me to accept that I was a battered wife on the run. It really didn't matter, though; I needed to be with my family and I wanted my children to be in a safe and comfortable environment, no matter what that would take. So I left him for good, moved in with my relatives and filed for a divorce.

I started going back to church regularly. One Sunday I remember my pastor speaking about the importance of getting an education and how God wanted for His people to live in prosperity. Although I had not had an education or lived the prosperous life that he was describing, I really believed that it was possible for me, so I listened intently. It was one of the most inspirational messages that I had heard up until that time. At last I had a hope of beginning my life all over again.

I took action and returned to school. This time would be far different than before. This time I was determined to finish school. During the day I worked and at night I cared for my children when I wasn't studying. I successfully completed the coursework, received my GED and got my first office job. My self-esteem began to grow. If I could get a GED, then I could also go to college. I began taking college courses and in time

I received a Bachelor of Arts degree in Human Services Management.

My new educational accomplishment gave me confidence to believe that life could be something beautiful once again. I actually felt like I was ready to give love a try one more time. My new friend was truly a kind gentleman. He loved being with my children. He always kept a job and at times helped me with my shopping, my cooking and the cleaning. He faithfully attended church with me and even sang with a local gospel group. I felt there was great possibility for a wonderful marriage and future. We had one child together, and he proved to be a wonderful father. But I realized that I still wasn't ready yet.

I still needed to be delivered from my fear of physical abuse. I was hurting inside. Although I had a degree and was doing far better than I had ever done before, I still suffered from low self-esteem. Deep down within I realized that I was not mentally or physically ready for a new relationship or a new marriage. My innermost being was crying out to be loved, but the kind of love that I needed was the unconditional love that no human could supply.

Around this time my sister joined another local church in the area. She had a wonderful glow about her, a positive attitude and a love for the Word of God. Watching her example made me realize that I was missing something in my Christian walk with the Lord. She invited me to go to church with her and I did. She walked me right down to the front of the church. I was so used to sitting in the back of churches that I was not sure if I was ready to sit so near to the pastor, a man so close to God.

As the pastor spoke, I immediately discovered what I was missing. I was so used to being a victim that I never took time to ask the Holy Spirit to come into my life. I realized that I lacked the power of the Holy Spirit. I knew then that I could not live one more day without the baptism of His Spirit. I clearly remember when the Spirit of the living God fell upon me. When I started to speak in tongues I first wanted to pull back because it seemed as if I was having an out-of-body experience.

There was a strong pulling of my spirit. I quickly relaxed and the power of the Holy Spirit flowed out of me. A change came over me like I had never before experienced. I prioritized my time. My personal relationship with Christ came first; my family came next. Next was my career, and then I began to focus on establishing real friendships. Each came in the order of priority listed. God completely healed me as He began the daily work of transforming me.

In the transformation process one of the greatest things that I learned was that I had to forgive others. When I forgave, it would turn into a major internal healing for myself. Realizing the delivering power of forgiveness, I began to write letters and make phone calls to my ex-husband and my former friends, forgiving them and asking them for forgiveness. My deliverance had truly begun.

For six years I submitted to my pastor. I strictly followed the principles he taught and applied them to my life. Although I had come a long way, I still was not who God wanted me to be. I asked forgiveness and extended my forgiveness to others. But I had not forgiven myself; nor did I see myself as God saw me. I had not tapped into my full potential because I had not let go of the guilty feelings and feelings of low self-esteem.

Pastor Dickerson taught me to recognize that God had created me in His image and that there was greatness within me. "You are no longer a victim," he would say. After hearing those words over and over again, they became real to me. Today I am fully convinced that I can do all things through Christ who strengthens me. I went on to graduate school and earned a Master's degree in Education. In the same year, I started my own business. I qualified to purchase my first home. Also, I became a licensed minister.

How did all these things happen for me? First, I believe in obeying my pastor. I believe in attending church regularly to combine my faith with other believers in corporate worship. As a trusted servant of God, I believe in returning my tithes and giving my talent and my time unconditionally to further the work of our ministry.

I believe in consistently attending Bible study so that I will always be learning and growing. These were all practical things that I would do and still do to keep my mind, body and soul focused on Christ. By doing those things it makes it difficult for the enemy to fill your mind with limiting beliefs. I'm free from abusive relationships forever. Now I seize every opportunity that I can to grow continually.

I Found My Demons Under the Bed

Lee's Confessions

❧

Dear friends, I urge you, as aliens and strangers in the world, to abstain from sinful desires, which war against your soul (1 Peter 2:11).

Sweeping under the bed on Saturdays was one of my first household chores. Since I was new to the household, I knew I had to do my chores if I wanted to stay there in my aunt's good graces. One day while doing my weekend chores, I uncovered pictures of naked women under my older cousin's bed. I was only 11 years old at the time and I kept my cousin's secret to myself. Just a few years shy of adolescence, I was curious about those nasty magazines.

Every Saturday when I dusted and cleaned cobwebs, I looked at the pictures of nude centerfolds in magazines that are usually hidden behind the counters at the neighborhood corner stores. The pictures reminded me of the first time that I caught one of my relatives having sex. They were caught right in the very act and I was only five years old. I didn't tell anybody what I'd seen because the sexual games they were playing looked fun and I wouldn't have wanted anyone to end my puerile fantasy.

To act out my fantasy, I started practicing what I saw them doing with my sister's naked dolls. By the time I was about seven years old, I started looking up little girls' dresses. My fetish was for girls with long skinny legs who wore fitted bikini panties under their short dresses. It would have been one thing if it stopped there, but it didn't. My obsession for naked women became my next speculation, and that was risky. I remember getting caught peeking under the bathroom stalls in a bathroom.

When at home, I would take many of my cousin's magazines and flip through the pages devouring all the colorful pictures while I was supposed to be taking a bath. The bathroom became my sanctuary for new sexual fantasies. I'd sit on the toilet masturbating while looking at the pornographic images. When I was about 13, I accidentally walked into a room where I unexpectedly found one of my uncle's friends watching a pornographic movie.

To my surprise, the man didn't turn the movie off, but teased me about it. "You don't know anything about that, huh?" I was shocked. The images on the TV screen showed men who were having sex with more than one woman at a time, performing oral sex on each other, and all kinds of other illicit sexual acts that I had never seen before. My mouth flung open as wide as ever. I felt like I had graduated. I'd been promoted. The movie was better than any centerfold I'd seen in the magazines. The dirty movie made me anxious to see more sex videos. A whole new door was opened wide for me to explore.

One day after school, a friend struck up a conversation about beautiful naked women. Connecting with his conversation, I told him about the dirty movies that I'd seen. "Oh, I have plenty of those," he bragged. I couldn't contain my excitement. "You have plenty of those? How did you get them?" His friend said his older brother let him watch skin movies as much as he'd like to.

All of us were only about 13 years old or so, and we became totally obsessed with the films. I couldn't control my appetite for the movies that my friend showed me. They were simply not enough to satisfy my ever-growing desires. I found a way to get more from the black market. I had a borrowed collection combined with my new finds of pornographic movies stashed right next to the magazines that I'd found in my cousin's underwear drawer. He did not get caught, so I figured that I wouldn't either. It seemed like a safe place to hide my stash.

Every chance I got I masturbated. My lust for pornography held my undivided attention all the way into my adult years. Even when I tried to have girlfriends, my relationships were never very meaningful or normal. I always needed something more, more than they'd be willing to give. My search led me to gentlemen's clubs where the women danced completely nude on stage. The Internet opened up an entirely new world to view more pornography. So there you have it, my world was consumed with naked women.

Some men read the *Wall Street Journal*, The Robb Report, *Sports Illustrated* magazine, *National Geographic*, or *Time* magazine. Not so with me; I went to work with pornographic literature in my lunch box. During my break, while my co-workers ate lunch, I looked at pornographic literature and made 1-900 calls to sexually explicit phone lines for my lunch.

One day a co-worker, who noticed my addictive habit, started talking to me about the Lord, the last thing that I wanted to hear about. I had always avoided church because I felt that I didn't really need church. Although I initially shrugged off the conversation, I thought about what the young man had said to me about his need to give his life to the Lord, his own conversion experience. On my way home I couldn't help but keep thinking about what my co-worker said, "You need peace, and true peace can only come through Jesus Christ."

For whatever reason, I started sleeping restlessly for many nights. To ease my restlessness, I would get up to make pornographic phone calls, even though I knew that I could barely afford my regular monthly phone bill. Never before had I allowed myself to think about how I could not maintain a meaningful relationship, I always tried to use pornographic literature and pornographic videos to spice up my relationships with young ladies and that turned most women off, at least the decent women. Now I began to reflect on my actions.

Women thought I was very strange and very weird, and they rejected me. There was an aura about me that they instinctively picked up on. My battle with pornographic images continued to take over my mind. When I wanted female companionship, I decided to hire a prostitute, but I didn't have enough money to even pay her. I was a mess.

This became an eye-opener for me and I knew that I was going to need professional help.

Totally depressed and unhappy, I sought counseling, hoping that it would free me from my problem. My problem got so bad that I became lethargic, so much so that I started to miss days from work, something I had never done before. Knowing that something was obviously wrong, my supervisor told me straightforwardly that I needed to get help for whatever I was going through. I was a bit ashamed to confess, so I didn't tell him that pornography was ruining my life.

At night I would try to sleep but couldn't because the pornographic images crowded into my dreams. Believe it or not, my addiction intensified after I got professional counseling. It seemed as if the evil spirits got mad at me for seeking out help and urged me even more to watch movies and to flip through pages uncovering the newest centerfolds. As if I had a quota, I was determined to watch a certain amount of videos a week. I could not sleep, eat or work until I had my fill.

By the end of that week I cried out. I really didn't know why I was crying, but I did know that I was at my wits' end. The following week I met the same co-worker who told me about the peace that I needed in Jesus Christ. Curious, I asked the young man how he got saved. My co-worker told me about how God delivered him from a lifestyle of gangbanging and drug dealing. I began to think about this guy and how he was delivered from these things. I thought to myself if God could deliver him from his violent and destructive lifestyle, then perhaps He could deliver me too.

"Well, I need to be delivered from what I'm going through," I said. Pornography had taken over my life. I never second-guessed where this need came from or what it actually meant to be delivered. Suddenly, the things I saw as a child started coming back to me very vividly. My co-worker told me about a revival that was going on at his church and I decided to go. God ministered a powerful word through a guest preacher. It was just what I needed.

That very night I decided to give my life to the Lord. I wept uncontrollably and started vomiting up what I now realize was the aftermath of evil spirits inside of me. While I was on my knees on the floor and I looked like a pitiful mess, I asked God to deliver me. One of the ministers told me, "Whatever it is that's holding you back, just release it and give it up to the Lord. Call it out and confess these things." I began to quietly call out certain things.

The brethren standing nearby laid their hands on me and commanded the demonic spirits of pornography and the demonic spirits of sexual perversion to loose their hold on me, and they rebuked the enemy out of my life, out of my mind and out of my will. From that very moment God miraculously set me free.

I was set free by the power of God. Although I've had a few times when I slipped up since I was first delivered, my pastor taught me how to take my problem back to the Lord and receive His cleansing over again. I can honestly say that it has been years now and I have been totally free. Now I walk in total deliverance without pornography binding me up, causing me to lose sleep, money and meaningful relationships.

Today I am engaged in a meaningful relationship. Instead of wasting my money on magazines, videos or cyber-sex, I am able to utilize my money wisely. Strong and healthy relationships take on a whole new meaning for me now; I am getting married and planning to rear a family. My desire is to be the best father I can be to my little son and to be a responsible and accountable husband to my wife. Before, all those things would have only been a dream. Now I feel I can do these things since I've been set free by the power of God.

If you struggle in this area, you too can be delivered from pornography. You can be delivered from sexual perversion. Any sexual demons and sexual temptations that haunt you and try to drag you down are not stronger than the power of God. One thing that I will not do is to try to make excuses for my behavior by saying that "I was sick." I fully recognize that my behavior was totally irresponsible and I really cannot truthfully blame anyone but myself.

Now I walk in the fear, nurture, admonition and favor of God because I decided one night to go to a revival that forever changed my life. At this writing I am enrolled in Bible school and faithfully serving in the church. For the first time in my life I am at peace with myself, at peace with my fiancée, at peace with my little son and, most importantly, at peace with God.

If you suffer from this same problem, don't make any excuses. Don't wait until it gets worse and becomes destructive. Run to the altar. That altar can be in your bedroom, your church, somewhere else in your house, a city street corner, or with somebody ministering to you. Your altar is your place of deliverance. Get to your place of deliverance so that God can begin your process. Make yourself accountable to someone who is stronger than you are and begin to live a productive and purpose-filled life.

God Unlocked My Prison Walls

The Liberating Story of Minister Monterial Bynoe

❧❧❧

The Spirit of the Lord is on me, because he has anointed me to preach good news to the poor. He has sent me to proclaim freedom for the prisoners and recovery of sight for the blind, to release the oppressed (Luke 4:18).

I had just handed off a package when the police stepped out of the elevator. It took them only a few minutes before their hands were all over me. Of course, they found the rest of my drugs hidden in a "private area." Before I knew it, I was in the back of a cruiser on my way to the precinct to get booked. That was my very first weekend in jail. Like most guys in jail, I found Jesus. As the other guys in the cell slept restlessly, I quietly stayed up and prayed to God. I promised, "If You get me out of this, I won't do it again."

My mother was 17 when she gave birth to me. She raised me in Orchard Park, the toughest and most feared public housing projects in the Roxbury section of Boston. That's were I got my training, where I learned to fight, to rip off gold chains, to pick pockets and to rob drunks when I needed some money for my own pockets. By the time I was 15 years old, I went from selling dime bags to bundles of heroin and cocaine. I was making more money in a day than my mother made in one week. Business became so lucrative that I thought it was almost unreal. Deep inside me I knew that it would only be a matter of time before the boys in blue would put me in handcuffs.

The streets were downright brutal. A drug war had broken out between the New York boys (aka Apple City) and the Detroit boys (aka Naked City). Like any war, people got killed right there on the city's streets. In this war people got killed for as little as a dime bag of weed, an unfair exchange for human life. Thinking back over it, my getting caught in that hallway for selling drugs with the intent to distribute probably saved my life.

While I was in jail, I found out that a guy from my crew was murdered. With that I promised God and myself that I'd stop selling drugs because I knew that I was not ready to die. I didn't stay in jail long. My mother always said if I got caught, she'd never let me rot in jail. By week's end, Mom bailed me out. About one year later I moved out of my mother's house thinking that it was time for me to be on my own.

I was about 16 years old. I had a son on the way, no job and no marketable skills because I had quit school to earn money. If only I had known that more trouble was already searching me out. One day I was at home just chilling out and minding my own business when my cousin came by and said, "Monty, get your gun." We had to go pay a visit to this guy who was beating up on two of my aunts. So I got my pistol.

This guy had given one aunt a black eye and broke my other aunt's jaw. Later on that night, I saw this same dude walking home. I ran up on him and asked, "Why did you hit my aunts?" I shot him twice at point-blank range in the chest and stomach. Luckily, he didn't die. But I was on the run from the police for attempted murder. My cousin was picked up and went to jail for another crime he had committed. Police also charged him with the attempted murder because he was with me when it happened.

All of my family was looking for me. My cousin's mother wanted me to turn myself in and tell the police my cousin had nothing to do with the shooting. I told her she must be out of her mind if she thought that I was going to do that. For about six months I laid low staying out of any real trouble. One day my friends came by and picked me up in a stolen car. I didn't really want to go with them, but I went anyway.

That was a big mistake. As we left the house and were riding down Morton Street, we got into a car accident. My friend driving the car was high, I mean, tore up. We left the scene and were on our way to Newton, Massachusetts, an elite suburb of Boston, to steal a newer car. We were in Newton trying to rip off a BMW. While we were trying to get into the car the lady who owned the car walked up to it. My friend jumped out of her car and got back into our car.

By this time, the police were following us around in a black Cadillac through Newton. All of a sudden, we had all kinds of police cars chasing us. We could hear the helicopter chasing us from above. There was no getting away from them. It was a cold and snowy November day. We jumped out of the car and ran through an unfamiliar town. Police were everywhere and we ran right under a bridge trying our best to escape.

The only options that we had at that present moment were to go to jail or swim. My friends said they were not going back to jail, so they jumped into the Charles River. I knew I didn't want to go jail either, so I jumped in too. All three of us were trying to swim in this freezing water. I remember swimming past one of my friends. Then I lost all my strength and started to go under. I was drowning. All of a sudden I heard a voice, which I recognize today as the Holy Spirit, that said, "Just stand up." When I did, I saw the other side of the river and I knew that I did not swim that far. God was protecting me when I did not even realize it.

Needless to say, I still got arrested. Sadly, one of my friends died in the river. At the police station, I gave the police an alias and they gave me $1,500 bail. I remember calling home and telling them to come and get me before they found out I had a warrant. As I was signing my release papers, the phone rang. To my surprise, it was the guy I had shot telling the police my real name and that I was wanted for attempted murder back in Boston. When the police got off the phone, they grabbed me and I was done. I spent that long weekend in the Roxbury police station.

That cell was the worst place to be. They would not give me clothes until I went to court that Tuesday morning. I ended up in the Charles Street Jail. I was there for five hours before my family posted my $1,500 bail. I spent two weeks at home waiting trial. During that time the police framed me for a murder. They said I was a part of a sting that had gone bad. A drug dealer from Miami was moving two kilos of cocaine to Boston and got robbed and was murdered in the process.

I would spend the next eight years of my life in prison. Only 18 years old, I made it to the big house, Walpole State Prison. My time in prison was hard at first because I had a real chip on my shoulder and I couldn't let anyone think I was weak. So I fought a lot and disrespected the correction officers. After one nasty brawl, the prison guards sent me back behind the wall, solitary confinement. It was then that I began to question God and ask, "Why do I always get caught up in stuff?"

I had been locked up for about a week when the Spirit of the Lord began to speak to me. I really thought I was going crazy. The Lord asked me questions I just could not answer. "What is your purpose? Why are you even alive today?" I realized I did not know the answers and no one was around to help answer these probing questions. The very next morning somebody slid a book under my door. I began to read and I could not stop reading it. The guy who gave me the book was just like me: a thief, a con man and a convict.

The only difference was he was serving 100 years and I was doing 10 to 15. The man had given his life to God. And God miraculously caused favor to happen in his life and released him early from that prison sentence. I finished reading the book which had a part that gave an invitation to know Jesus. I remember saying "yes" to the invitation. I read that sinner's prayer out loud. That was the beginning of my life in Christ Jesus. For the next two and a half years, I learned how to study the Word of God and to pray.

While in my prison cell I received the baptism of the Holy Spirit. Eventually I served my time and was released from prison. Upon my release from prison, I started attending church. One night a guest speaker at the church preached about the anointing of God and the power of God. I had seen preachers lay hands on people on television, but never in person. I said to God, "If this is real, I want to experience it for myself." All of a sudden, the preacher told us to praise God. I started praising God.

The preacher came over to me and began to pray in the Spirit. As he laid his hand on my forehead, I instantly went down under the power of God. After that experience with God, I decided to join the ministry. All along, I knew God had called me to preach the Word of God. I knew that God has delivered me from a life of crime to help other young men in their search for freedom.

Today I am preaching and teaching the Word of God. I am married with children, a homeowner and a productive member of society. The life that I am living was never a reality in my teenaged mind. But one thing I now realize is that true deliverance will not only free you from physical prison walls, but more importantly from the prison walls of your own mind.

They Abused Me Until I Broke

Name Witheld

❧

Do not love the world or anything in the world. If anyone loves the world, the love of the Father is not in him (1 John 2:15).

The two guys watched me bouncing my wide hips up and down during my lap dance. Afterwards they invited my friend and me to a disco party at New York's Studio 57. We accepted their invitation because the two guys promised us lots of cash and the time of our lives outside of Boston.

I lied to my parents about where I was going. I told them I was going to my girlfriend's house in Connecticut so they'd keep my kids. I promised to be back in three days. The New York club was spectacular. We stayed in a private room, drinking and smoking cocaine, until the men carried us out of there. I passed out in the car—and woke up in a nightmare.

Handcuffed to a radiator, naked and drugged, I watched in a haze as different men took turns on top of me. I held on for dear life, shaking with fear as their sweat covered my body. I felt dirty all over. Before I blacked out again, I begged for God's help. I woke up again and the men were gone. I yanked the cuffs until I broke free and ran out of the building, screaming for help. No one responded. I imagined the worst was to come. My mind was spinning. Yet, I held on to the fact that God had saved my life from certain death.

I snatched something to wear from the rack of clothes hanging in front of a store on the street. I covered my 25-year-old voluptuous body as a car pulled up beside me. I thought the kidnappers were back to kill me. But God sent His angels, an elderly couple from Boston, to drive me back to my hometown. I felt so safe in the couple's sedan that I curled up in the backseat and slept. They dropped me off at the YMCA in downtown Boston. They didn't ask me for money and openly wished that God would continue to protect me. My near-death experience ended quietly, but my dreams kept me up at night as I relived being raped twice before.

I was in grammar school when a wolf in sheep's clothing stole my virginity. Two of my third-grade classmates invited me over to their house to play after school. My mom let me go because the girls' father was a minister like my dad. She felt comfortable letting me play with his children after I told her they liked patty-cake and playing with dolls. It wasn't long before I learned that their father was not a holy man. The "preacher man" ruled with fear and prowled around his house for fresh prey once he closed his front door. He molested all the children in his house and I would be his latest victim. When his wife tried to stop him, he called her nasty names and raised his hand to slap her down as she reached for the telephone to call the police.

I had my first freeze frame moment as the man pulled up my dress and pulled my tights down to my knees. "What in the world is going on? What did I do to deserve this?" I could never tell my parents once I got home because I feared that they'd blame me. "Had I done something wrong?" As fresh tears streamed from my eyes, I gritted my teeth. He told me I couldn't tell. I thought of telling my father, a real man of the cloth. But my family didn't talk about such things in our home, which seemed like a sanctuary compared to that house of horrors. I remembered the preacher's cruel threats and his vicious words, and my vocal cords were paralyzed. I buried my hatred for the child molester deep inside. I didn't think of it again until I was about 16.

I was walking down the street when three guys, who'd been eyeing my shapely hips, grabbed me off the city street. They mistook me for an older woman, until my school badge fell out of my pocket. It didn't stop them, though. They took turns gang raping me as they covered my mouth to stop me from biting their thick callused palms. I wanted to die. When I broke free my body was so messed up that I stayed in the tub praying that my pain would wash down the drain with the dirty water. "Why did this thing happen to me?" After the preacher man stole my virginity when I was 7, I made sure I walked a certain way, trying to avoid attention from strange men. After being victimized for a second time, I felt like a hostage in my own body, so I stumbled down the path of drugs, alcohol and promiscuity. My slump lasted for the next five years.

I felt I had a chance to reverse my path when I met a local college student who became my lover. But our love didn't last. Our relationship soured as soon as our baby was born. He said my out-of-shape breasts and stretch marks disgusted him. His lips that used to shower me with wet kisses now spit nastiness as he took control over my life. I had to get away from the abuse, so I ran to my mother's house, where he showed up and promised to kill my son and me. He pulled a knife, put it to my throat and dared me to scream. My mom ran for the telephone and called the police, who forced him to leave.

I cooled out for a few days before I went back home. My crazy lover showed up for another showdown. I had had enough. When he raised his hand to me, I beat the living stew out of him with a baseball bat I hid under the bed. After he left, I erased my longing for him from my mind with alcohol and drugs.

After that relationship, I found other men who didn't treat me any better. My other baby's daddy was a drug dealer, hustler and abuser. In the beginning he bought me the best designer clothes and beautiful jewels to hang around my neck. I was so messed up on cocaine, though, that nothing satisfied me anymore. I slipped back into a loveless relationship. I was drowning. I lost control of my mind, body and soul, and he made me into his play toy while rock cocaine filled my emptiness. I gave this thug eight years of my life. Every time I ran for the door we fought, until one day I picked up my iron and struck him dead center between his eyes, "Wham!" My one-year-old child saw it all. His screams for his daddy forced me to recognize how far I'd sunk. "No, Mommy! No!" I looked at my child once more, but I needed to let this man know that he'd never put his hands on me again. I bashed him once more before I kicked him out of my house.

My anger reached a boiling point and I wanted all the men who'd violated me to pay. Some guys from the neighborhood found the preacher man who'd taken my virginity. I told them to stay in the car while I went around the house holding my .38 caliber revolver. I caught the preacher man by surprise and put the gun to his face. I forced him to look at me, when I noticed that the man who'd molested me so very long ago had lost his mind. He mumbled something unrecognizable and looked straight through me. His look frightened me as I slipped the gun back in my purse. His mental condition shook me up. As I walked away, God told me that this man had already paid the price for what he'd done to me 21 years ago.

When the angels who'd picked me up on the street in New York dropped me off at the "Y" in Boston, I knew I couldn't go back to swinging my naked body in exotic clubs. Instead I walked into a homeless shelter where they had a bed. When I wasn't staying there, I stayed with my mother and hid my addictions, which enslaved me. I spent my welfare check on booze, cigarettes and tranquilizers. I drank like crazy, smoked two and three packs of cigarettes a day, and popped pills to ease the pain.

I needed the bucks, but at 32 years old I couldn't go back to shaking my hips for money. I rededicated my life back to God. It was a different experience for me coming from my parents' beliefs. I remember my father baptizing me when I was young. At that time I accepted the Lord Jesus Christ as my personal Savior. But I did not understand or know what to do after that. Now as an adult I learned more fully about the things of God and His Spirit under the teachings of my pastor. God used my pastor to help me. I've learned so much about myself and who God is. This has been a blessing and has kept me sane. My life was full of mountains, valleys, forks in the road and turmoil. I've learned to walk with God and to maintain my relationship with Him by praying, fasting and studying His Word.

I was getting comfortable in the backseat of a cab on my way to church when I noticed the cab driver was one of the men I encountered in New York City. I was really scared. But I knew God was with me. It had been so many years and I didn't know if the cab driver recognized me. All I could think about was how good God has been to me. I shared the good news, grace and mercy of Jesus and how He came into my life. The cab driver was quiet for a while. He let me off at church. Before I got out of the cab, I examined the man's face and saw an old saggy-eyed man. I felt sorry for him as I parted with words God placed in my heart. "May God bless you and have mercy upon your soul."

At that moment I knew I had changed and become a true worshipper of God. At this time in my life, God wants me to build covenant relationships with people who are a part of my God-given destiny and purpose in life. He is calling me to be more discerning in whom I choose to have in my life. I can truly say that I am delivered from my past and the things that caused me to abuse myself. I truly thank God for saving me and delivering me from all these things that held me in bondage: the spirits of unworthiness, drugs, alcohol, promiscuity, fear, anger, abuse and pain. I prayed to God for total healing, deliverance and restoration, and He delivered me. I am now walking in total victory. I am more than a conqueror and I can do all things through Christ who strengthens me daily.

May God bless you and keep you under His wings always.

Forbidden Touches

Testimony of Kay

꧁꧂

Do you not know that the wicked will not inherit the kingdom of God? Do not be deceived: Neither the sexually immoral nor idolaters nor adulterers nor male prostitutes nor homosexual offenders nor thieves nor the greedy nor drunkards nor slanderers nor swindlers will inherit the kingdom of God. And that is what some of you were. But you were washed, you were sanctified, you were justified in the name of the Lord Jesus Christ and by the Spirit of our God (1 Corinthians 6:9-11).

As the preschoolers slept, Kay reached under their blankets to feel their private parts. "I'm just checking to see if she is wet."' It was a perfect cover. Not all the children were potty trained. Nobody wanted to deal with diaper rash. None of the other teachers suspected that Kay was a child molester. She applied for the job at the preschool not because she loved children, but because she needed an unsuspecting environment in which to feed her sexual appetite for small children.

She had been taught by the best. A latchkey kid, Kay's mother worked overtime to pay the bills and she was left home alone a lot. She was vulnerable and needy when her uncle came to live with them in southern Massachusetts. Her uncle was all too willing to take advantage. He was a Slick Willie who liked young girls. He showed Kay the tricks of a child molester who can easily fool a needy child with candy, games and hugs. Kay's uncle's game was making her into his sexual toy. For three years he did things to Kay that no adult should do to a child. Kay was no longer attractive to him once he stole her virginity. But she missed being touched. He had made the sex games fun.

She became a fast girl in high school. Every day after school Kay opened her window so boys in the neighborhood could climb inside the bedroom. Kay didn't care what they whispered behind her back. She thought the more the better. Her uncle had planted the seed that practice makes perfect. Whenever her mother was at work, she would let boys into her home and let boys have their way. She thought they loved her when they brought beer or liquor that made her relax. Her mother wasn't the wiser. She did not know that Kay was ruined by the inappropriate touches of her uncle and strange boys. She looked at Kay's bizarre behavior as the signs of a rebellious and defiant teenager.

By the time she was 16, Kay took a job baby-sitting for her mother's friend and she became a budding pedophile. The elementary school kids loved Kay because she liked playing hopscotch and jump rope with them. She wrestled with the boys and the girls and she touched them inappropriately. At night she would snuggle with them in bed and initiate sexual acts. She knew it was wrong when she went from fingering their genitals to actually having oral sex with some of the children. She never gave them money but rather things that every child enjoys: a new pair of sunglasses, balloons and toy cars. She took them out for pizza and to the park.

Later when she worked at the preschool, Kay felt the pain of what she had done and her past haunted her thoughts. She secretly wanted to be caught. She tried to shake off her sexual urges in her early 20s and tried not to touch children anymore. She started going to church and when she heard the Word of the Lord she felt convicted. But the evil spirits that haunted her tormented her mind. These spirits told her she'd never be free of her sexual urges to touch children. She resisted her urges and resigned from the preschool. She stopped being around small children. But she fantasized about little girls playing in the park.

At prayer meetings, her mind wondered. She didn't really know what it meant to be delivered, to be set free of the evil spirits, since at her church they talked about demons, deliverance, the gifts of the Spirit, and the power of God being manifested in daily living. Kay struggled with an enormous amount of guilt. She confessed to the wrong person. The person ended up telling it to someone else and this devastated Kay.

Kay confessed again at a prayer meeting. She caught the bug when other people in the group revealed embarrassing things about themselves. She told the group that evil spirits tormented her for more than 20 years. "I don't know

YOU TOO CAN BE DELIVERED

how to get free," she said. "I tried counseling. I tried talking to people. I can't get free."

Kay caught everyone at the meeting by surprise. Kay, the woman with the warm smile and an inviting personality, wasn't the person she pretended to be. Her confession was hard for them to believe. She told them how she wanted to commit suicide because of all the pain that she had inflicted upon other children.

After the meeting, she apologized to children and their parents. But the abuse had happened so long ago that many of the people she'd harmed were no longer around. One family took her to court. She was placed on probation and the judge ordered her into counseling. God showed her His favor and she was not sent to jail.

"I want to be totally free," she cried out to God during a meeting. She screeched and fell out on the floor. She squirmed on the floor and vomited right there in the meeting. The saints in the meeting cleaned her up. They prayed for God to cast out those unclean spirits that had kept Kay in bondage. It was a rough and tough situation. But Kay was delivered and set free by the power of God. The Lord set her free from the attacking spirits of pedophilia. He set her free from the spirits of molestation. Now Kay is married, has children and is leading a fruitful life. She is involved in her church.

Kay is living testimony that you too can be delivered from the demons of molestation and pedophilia. If you are bound by pedophilia, if you were a victim of pedophilia, you can be delivered. Just as God delivered Kay, He can deliver you too. You too can be delivered by the awesome power of God that is waiting to set you free, even now.

It's important, vitally important, to confess to one another when we sin against one another. If you wrong someone by taking his or her money, you confess it and say, "Please forgive me." That is the road toward being set free. If you have sinned against a young lady by sleeping with her before marriage, fornicating with her, then when you realize that you don't want to continue to do wrong and you come to yourself, you need to ask that young lady to forgive you.

If you're in church and say you are a member and yet are not a tither, you are a "skipper" or a "tipper." You need to be able to say, "Listen, I have not been doing it the right way. I have not been yielding to God. I have not been tithing. I need to ask God to forgive me, but also I need to ask my leader, my pastor, to forgive me, and then I need to move on." And you move on by not doing that what was wrong, but by doing what is right.

God Has Not Given Us the Spirit of Fear

Testimony of Mae

❦

Reflect on what I am saying, for the Lord will give you insight into all this (2 Timothy 2:7).

Mae could never figure out how to stop her parents from arguing. They were so relentless with their verbal assaults that Mae had trouble finding a safe haven anywhere in her house. The sounds of their voices paralyzed her with fear. She was so afraid of what might happen to one of them during their routine arguments that she could hardly breathe. Her mother yelled at her father and he yelled back. They went back and forth violently screaming, creating an atmosphere of fear.

She became so terrified that she would hide under her bed hoping the mattress and box springs would shelter her from the unfolding drama spiraling around her. When their violent words became insufficient, they would start throwing dishes, breaking them against the kitchen wall. If that wasn't enough, they would ball up their fists and go heads up. Mae's parents seemed to enjoy fighting one another.

While Mae tried her best to stay out of the line of fire, she watched, frozen in fear, as her father beat up her mother so badly that he put her in the hospital. Her mom barely survived that horrible attack. Her father went to prison for the brutal beating. Mae's mother nearly lost her life but survived by a miracle. Now that her dad was out of the picture Mae thought there would be peace in the household. To her surprise, she became the new target of her mother's regular assaults. The yelling and arguing in the house continued.

Mae lived in a state of continuous fear. Her self-esteem was so frayed that she hung her head low, never making eye contact with anyone. She found it difficult to share her thoughts with others. Any interaction with people was a dreaded experience for Mae. She felt worthless when she faced others and always expected to be hurt by them. Fear continually gripped her mind and she was unable to speak up for herself. She was constantly reminded and tormented when she thought of the many times that she was verbally abused and rejected.

Mae's mom left her home alone for days on end. At times she didn't know if her mom was dead or alive. She developed a sense of abandonment, which often left her in a constant state of alarm and emotional unrest. Fear pushed her into a state of chronic depression at the young age of 19. During this vulnerable stage in her life, Mae met an older man who treated her far better than anyone she'd ever met up until that point in her life. He bought things for her and made her feel good about herself. Things started to look up for Mae.

However, she soon became pregnant and moved in with her newfound lover. Since she never really had a genuine relationship with her mother, it made it all the more easy for her to leave home without having any strings attached. To her total surprise, once the baby was born, the man whom Mae thought was her knight in shining armor kicked her and their baby out on the streets for no legitimate reason.

All of a sudden he decided that he did not want a family. As if the inevitable were a common practice in her life, Mae was living once again in a state of perpetual abandonment. After this, Mae found herself homeless. She looked seemingly everywhere for a place to stay, roaming like a vagabond from homeless shelter to homeless shelter. Not able to cope with her inveterate reality, Mae began to use drugs. The drugs quickly caused her to lose control of her life. Her drug of choice was crack cocaine, which immediately caused her to become addicted. She became a functional addict. Because of her new habit Mae had to search diligently for the much-needed provision for herself and her child.

Her baby's daddy clearly did not want to help her with child expenses and cares, leaving her to carry the total load of rearing this child on her own. With no other recourse, Mae became a stripper in a nightclub. It was the only thing that would bring in the kind of money that she needed to make ends meet. And after all, nobody else wanted to help her, so she had to do whatever it would take just to survive. Stripping became her means of survival.

Like two winds passing each other by, Mae met a young lady who had previously shared the same pain. This young woman invited Mae to a support group at her church. Mae had never stepped foot in a church before but decided that she would give it a try considering she had nothing to lose. In this support group she met many people from different walks of life who also were survivors of traumatic experiences. Mae shared her story with them and wept openly about her fears. She decided to join the church but she really did not get saved. There were times that she didn't feel comfortable there.

Because of her own complex, she thought that the church members talked behind her back about how she dressed and her timid nature. Mae was so imprisoned by her fears that she left the church. Again, Mae began to live her life on the run, from one place to another, from one relationship to the next relationship. After two years of living in total chaos, at the young age of 21, Mae decided to reconnect with the sister from the church who had invited her to the support group.

The woman expressed her concern about Mae's salvation. "You're not at peace with God," she told Mae. The woman gave Mae some Christian literature to read. She went home and read the tracts, which convicted her heart and caused her to cry out, "God, help me!" After that meeting, God answered her prayers. Mae was blessed with a nice apartment almost immediately. Although Mae was still struggling to provide for her daughter, she decided to give up her life in the streets. She started going back to church, but she did not totally yield to the Lord.

Going to church was Mae's only outlet, which was a great blessing for her. The downside was that Mae was still paralyzed with fears. She was always paranoid and afraid every night before she went to sleep. Acting on her fears, she locked her doors and put chairs up against them to make sure no one could come into her house and hurt her.

Her dreaded thoughts convinced her that someone was breaking into her house to kidnap her. Frightened and persuaded by the illusory reality of these imaginary thoughts, she often called 911 for help. She realized that no matter how hard she tried that she would never be able to live in peace without divine intervention. No longer able to deal with her fears, she pleaded once again, "God, please help me!"

The very next morning, Mae reached for the telephone after watching an episode of *The 700 Club* on TV. One of the telephone counselors ministered to her and told her that she could be delivered and set free. After her conversation with them, she called up the young sister from the church that ministered to her from time to time and asked her how she could be delivered from her fears. Mae flooded her with questions. "Can God deliver me from low self-esteem, abuse, hurt and rejection? Can God deliver me from fear?" For each of her questions the lady confidently let her know that God could help her in all of these areas if she would allow Him to.

The sister, who'd patiently ministered to her, periodically visited Mae in her apartment with several other sisters from her church. They talked to Mae about deliverance and shared with her various scriptures in the Bible that dealt with deliverance. Mae began to weep inwardly until it became noticeable on the outside. The sisters laid their hands on her and began to pray for her in the Name of the Lord Jesus Christ. Mae tried to push them off, as she was resisting the urge to stop the prayer, when a demonic screech came out of her mouth shouting, "I will not let her go!"

"Leave her alone!" persisted the demonic voice within. Mae started crying more intensely. These praying women started rebuking the enemy as the power of the Holy Spirit began to fill Mae's apartment. Mae felt the power of God move as she violently shook while the evil spirits that controlled her mind were being cast out. Mae asked God to forgive her of all the things that she had done wrong, including harboring spirits of fear.

They ministered to Mae late into the midnight hour, continuously crying out to God to deliver her and set her free. That very day Mae gave her life to the Lord. Since that conversion, fear has never had dominion over her anymore. Mae began to use the spoken Word of God as her weapon of choice against the spirit of fear. She quoted such Bible verses as, *"There is no fear in love. But perfect love drives out fear, because fear has to do with punishment. The one who fears is not made perfect in love"* (1 John 4:18) and *"You will keep in perfect peace him whose mind is steadfast, because he trusts in you"* (Isaiah 26:3). First John 4:18 became one of her favorite verses.

When the enemy told her that she wasn't going to stay saved and that she wasn't going to make it, she would use the Word of God as her defense. She spoke the Word aloud. *"To him who is able to keep you from falling and to present you before his glorious presence without fault and with great joy— to the only God our Savior be glory, majesty, power and authority, through Jesus Christ our Lord, before all ages, now and forevermore! Amen"* (Jude 24-25).

Even though Mae knew she was free from the bondage of fear, her panic attacks would occasionally return. But one day she was looking for answers and walked up to the altar for prayer after hearing the minister's message about life and death being in the power of the tongue. She accepted the message as the truth that she needed for her walk in total deliverance. The minister told her that the Lord had secured a way for her to maintain her deliverance by quoting the Word of God, by standing on what God says and by confessing deliverance daily.

Little did she know before how powerful confession actually was. Her deliverance could have been actualized long before this moment had she only known that she had the power over her life in her own mouth. With that, Mae began to rejoice, weep and express unrestrained thanks to God because she realized that she had actually been delivered. Today Mae no longer faces any of her past battles with fear. All her fears have been totally conquered and surrendered to the Lordship of Jesus the Christ.

Mae boldly witnesses about the goodness and glory of God without any feeling of timidity, for she knows firsthand what the mighty power of God can do as we yield ourselves to Him. She has met people who have experienced her same trouble and were delivered. Mae maintains her deliverance and empowers other women to do the same through her prayer life, quoting scriptures, standing on the Word of God and confessing deliverance daily. God gave Mae peace and now she is able to share peace with others.

Mae's testimony should encourage every believer or non-believer who has been plagued with spirits of fear. What do you fear? What plagues you on a daily basis? Has the enemy convinced you that you would always fail? Are you afraid of going back to school? Driving a car? Entering into a meaningful relationship? Do you fear your past or your future?

Whatever your fear, you need to know that God will deliver you from the spirit of fear just like God delivered Mae. If you will dare to confess the Word that God spoke concerning your strength and total victory, He will break the bonds of the enemy that so desires to keep you in a state of trepidation. The enemy cannot have you. The blood of Jesus Christ, the Lamb of God, has already purchased you if you are saved. And wherever He is there will always be perfect peace.

A Cinderella Story

Testimony of Sister B

❧

Dear friends, let us love one another, for love comes from God. Everyone who loves has been born of God and knows God (1 John 4:7).

"From the time I was very small I always believed that I was a dunce, no more than a fool. My mother started drilling those feelings into me when I was only seven. She and my stepfather treated me like Cinderella (the fairy-tale child who was forced to labor for her sisters and mother), forcing me to cook and clean for them and my brothers and sisters. Without receiving a maid's compensation I slaved around the house performing all the domestic chores no one else wanted to do. Although I was my mother's biological child, I surely felt like a stepchild.

"My mother used to beat me like a master beats his slave. The food I worked so hard to prepare was always burnt, she said, and the house was never clean enough to meet her lofty standards. I was no stranger to name-calling; I was regularly called 'a dunce and a fool' while my mom would repeatedly whip my frail little legs. Like a doctor on call, I was always at my mother and stepfather's beck and call.

"My stepfather would at times demand me to bring him some water, and when I did, he would kick me hard, like I was a dog. At other times he would slip into the kitchen while I was washing dishes and grab me from behind and fondle my tiny adolescent breasts. 'Stop! Leave me alone!' I told him, hoping my mother would intervene. My mother would come into the kitchen replying, 'What's the matter?' Totally afraid that I would get a greater punishment if I told, I chose to keep my mouth shut. After all, he told me that if I told I would get in a whole heap of trouble. If I told her, I'd still lose."

Sister B felt that her mother never loved her or even liked her for that matter. As a child she would envision her mother showing her love and affection by allowing her to sit on her lap and telling her how pretty she looked in her dress; the kind of affirmation other little girls received from their mothers. Needless to say, those dreams never came to pass. Instead her mother's demeaning and cruel words were her reality.

Sister B stopped dreaming altogether and her hopes of becoming a school teacher someday vanished into the night. Having been inculcated with so many negatives all her life, she began to think that she was incapable of living the so-called good life, whatever that meant. Sister B did not have a real concept of the value of life even after all the abusiveness ceased. Perhaps the damage was too far gone. She began to see herself and view her life as simply meaningless. Added to that was the inevitable silent killer of low self-esteem, of which she had an abundant supply.

At the young age of nine years when most children are daydreaming about what they are going to receive on their birthday or who's coming over to play with them, Sister B had a serious bout with major depression. Sister B started having suicidal thoughts that would haunt her almost every day. She rampaged and raved around the house searching for something to put her out of her misery. Finally she found a bottle of aspirin and, hoping that it would permanently take away her pain, guzzled every pill down without hesitation. That did not work. So after that attempt failed, she tried to stab herself to death. Again she was unsuccessful. But she was persistent and continued.

When Sister B's mother wanted to give her a whipping, she told her to go outside and get a "switch," a branch of one of the bushes outside. Sister B thought that this was her golden opportunity to help her mother kill her; something that she thought would make her mother happy. Most children, when asked to get their switch, often try to get the very smallest twig of a switch they can find. Not so for Sister B. She went out and got a branch with the long sharp thorns attached, hoping that the thorns would literally rip her tender flesh apart.

As she ripped the branches from the tree, she felt confident that her torture would end in death, something that she really desired. *I'm going to help Mom get rid of me*, she thought. She stood totally vulnerable and stark naked anticipating the one of many strikes that would be the final blow ushering her to her final resting place. With every strike she endured she told God, "Lord, if You don't let me kill myself, let her do it. And if she doesn't kill me, then let her get hit by a car or something. I just can't bear this anymore!"

When Sister B was 12 years old, her mother left home to attend her cousin's funeral. That was the last time she saw her mother alive. Just as she prayed for, a speeding 18-wheeler truck tragically killed her mom. The next morning, Sister B and her siblings woke up to the devastating news about their mom. An overwhelming numbness came over her. Sister B's response was nonchalant and somewhat mystifying. Silently she vowed to herself that she would not allow another person to abuse her.

Shortly after her mom's death Sister B dropped out of school. She started to become sexually permissive and got pregnant two times both while she was in her teenage years. Now carrying the responsibility of a single mother without adequate education and at only 19 years old, Sister B started drinking heavily as her way of escaping from her reality. Being totally out of control of herself when she would drink, she often found herself in strange places and in compromising situations.

She recalls, "I remember one time waking up in a local park with my clothes torn off, later to discover that I had been drugged, badly beaten and raped." One problem just led to another. Sister B started using heroin and cocaine. She thought drugs would make her feel better. Instead the pain became almost unbearable. The drugs did not ease the pain and hurt at all; they only intensified the pain.

All she wanted was an escape from her past. She had a sizable hole in her life and was determined to fill it. What she really wanted was love, but she did not have a foggy clue on what love was or where she could actually find it. For Sister B love was someone telling her that she was pretty, that she was worthwhile, and that she possessed quality attributes like compassion.

In her futile search for love Sister B lost so much. She lost her self-respect all in search of companionship. She would let both men and women use her. Sister B would do stupid stuff just to gain their approval, and they would simply laugh and talk about her. Although her so-called friends were mistreating her, she would continue to stay around them because she was so love-deficient that she would rather be around somebody even if he was abusive. She just wanted to be loved, and having friends around her at least appeared to be love.

All of the unkind things they said to her she took out on herself. She looked into her bathroom mirror, crying and repeating all the nasty affirmations that her mother had taught her, "You're ugly. You're stupid. Nobody loves you. Nobody wants you." She remembers asking God to help her. "If I could just get somebody to really love me; if I could just get somebody to hold me, I would be all right." She sort of made a bargain with God. "God, I'll give up the drinking and drugs if You will give me someone to love."

The problem is that the things she promised herself did not last. She continued to get drunk and high. In fact, it even got worse. She would start selling her body just to support her drug and alcohol habit. Realizing that she could not responsibly rear her two children in the condition that she was in, she sent her children down south to live with their father. That was obviously a better choice for the sake of the children. However, the absence of her children caused her to take an introspective look at herself, birthing a fresh batch of feelings of pain, loss and despondency.

After her fifth overdose on a heroin and cocaine cocktail, she stopped getting high for about seven months. She woke up one morning and heard a voice inside saying, "If you get high today, you're going to die." Sister B remembered reaching for the telephone that morning and calling the Dimmock Community Health Center, a rehabilitation center for people who give up taking drugs. Although she was completely off the heroin, they asked her to come in anyway.

About three or four weeks after that, an old friend called to offer a tempting proposition. "I got some good stuff. You wanna get high?" She said, "Oh, yeah!" Just like that Sister B totally forgot about the good people who accepted her into Dimmock; she forgot about everybody. The way she looked at it was that she needed something to dull the pain. The pain was too deep for her to bear. As she was riding on the train to meet him, she began crying. Although one side of her really wanted to get high, she just could not carry it out. So she went with her inner strength and went back to Dimmock.

Back at Dimmock, she tried winding down by smoking a cigarette and quickly discovered that she had lost a taste for the nicotine also. She was becoming a different person. The next week some sisters from a local church had Bible study with some of the people at the center. They read the Bible, ministered to Sister B about Jesus, and asked if anyone wanted prayer. Sister B was one of the first to raise her hand.

Those women prayed over her, quoted the sinner's prayer with Sister B repeating each word, and she accepted Christ that day. She began to cry aloud! Something on the inside of her had truly changed, although she really couldn't describe it. One of the women invited her to church and Sister B confessed, "I would like to go, but I have nothing to wear." That problem was overcome instantly as one of the sisters of the church blessed her with an outfit to wear to the service.

She recalls that as she walked into the church, "I felt the Spirit of the Lord as the congregation worshipped in song. I stood up and clapped my hands and something knocked me down to the floor. I stood back up and was knocked down again. This time I remained on the floor weeping and crying out to the Lord. When I recovered from the life-changing experience the pastor asked, 'Who wants to be saved?' I ran up to the altar knowing that I had just experienced the power of God saying, 'I got it! I got it! I got it, now!' That day was the beginning of my life."

For years she was in bondage, but now at age 42 Sister B experienced freedom like she had never experienced in all her life. She readily admits that she had given her life to the Lord yet still lacked understanding. Her childhood had obscured her ability to properly cope with problems. Sister B could not fix her own life overnight and make it all better again. But the one thing that she could do was to attend church faithfully, and that she would not stop doing.

She always viewed herself as nobody until she received from the Word that we are all fearfully and wonderfully made in the image of God. Sister B now shares her testimony with people everywhere she goes, telling about the loving power of Jesus Christ. Being a servant all her life, she understood the concept of serving. However, it was not until she began to become a disciple that she understood that being a servant yields rewards in this life and in the life to come.

Sister B now realizes that God has been a part of her life since she was a child, although she didn't realize it then. There is not a single day that goes by that she does not thank God for bringing her the freedom that only His power could bring. Although many people believe that once an addict always an addict, it has been 13 years now and Sister B is drug free. She serves on the Missionary Board at her church.

God Gave Me a New Identity

Testimony of Deacon Ron Bell

❧

You were taught, with regard to your former way of life, to put off your old self, which is being corrupted by its deceitful desires; to be made new in the attitude of your minds; and to put on the new self, created to be like God in true righteousness and holiness (Ephesians 4:22-24).

Long before actor Wesley Snipes and other dark-skinned black actors became Hollywood sex symbols, my hard-to-comb nappy hair and black skin centered me as the target of taunts and racial slurs. Mean-spirited lighter-skinned black people made fun of me, calling me names like "blackie" and "tar baby" as they passed me on the streets in Boston's

87

Mission Hill section. I didn't make my skin the color that it is, yet they made me feel like I had a disease.

The "sticks and stones may break your bones" rhyme promised that names would never hurt you. As a little boy, I could not stop questioning why these things were happening to me. My parents were hard workers who encouraged all their six children to be the best that we could be in life. My father, a disabled veteran, was still able to work two full-time jobs as a welder and a baker. My mother worked as a bus monitor and a community organizer and activist.

We all were very active in the Salvation Army Church. I played in the band both in the army and in our high school band. But no matter where I was, I always stuck out in our race-conscious environment as if I were a leper. Whether I was at school, in church or on the streets with my friends hanging out, I was always the darkest one in the bunch. Because of that I always struggled with loving myself for who I was. I hated my skin, hair and even the body that I was born with.

If only black people jeered at me it would be one thing, but white people would pick on me also because of the way I looked. I can remember walking through the neighborhood on my way to my Cub Scout meetings when I was about nine years old and three guys waited for me to pass on the street so they could spit on me. Their spit was always mixed in with what they were drinking, so I often went to my Cub Scout meetings with the horrible smell of liquor on me.

Later I started attending the prestigious Boston Latin High School and I was the only African American person in most of my classes. It felt really awkward having to learn under those conditions, particularly since some of my teachers made fun of me and called me racist names. Adults, children, blacks and whites all making fun of me added to the pressure that I already faced within me of not loving and embracing who I was and what I looked like. It started to overwhelm me.

While all this was going on, my family had to deal with my older brother's issues. My older brother was a drug dealer who would not learn his lesson on the first go around. He would get caught repeatedly dealing drugs, yet wind up selling them all over again. That would continue until he got caught and sent to prison, bringing shame and embarrassment on my parents' hard-working heritage.

My father used to work so hard that he was hardly home. That of course did not help my situation at all. I was a growing boy who needed my father just to talk to about some of the things that were on my heart. Yet the impression that I gathered from him is that they had more important things to deal with than me airing out my emotional insecurities.

Nobody wanted to hear me, so I found my solace when I started smoking dope. And it was great. I mean it really did the job. Smoking my first marijuana joint, I felt oblivious to all the jeering and critical remarks spewed out at me every time I stepped outside. Even though I was lost and friendless, I ended up bonding with some of the older guys. They treated me like a dog, just like the others, but I kept hanging with them because I was looking for older male role models in my life.

By the time I finished high school, I was an angry young black man. Church did not seem to address my problems in a personal way so I really did not feel the need in continuing to go anymore. I thought that I would do a whole lot better in life if I could just get out of Boston. And that is exactly what I did as I headed for college to the city of brotherly love, Philadelphia. At first, everything seemed to be okay.

I was playing basketball and making the dean's list, yet still I used cocaine. To earn some money on the side, I began to sell drugs. To me my life was under control. After all, I was doing better than I had ever done before and was not exposed to the same peer group I grew up around. Still, I had this constant nagging feeling inside that told me there was something missing in my life.

After finishing college, I returned to Boston to pursue a higher degree in business. The strange thing is that I still used cocaine and alcohol to fill the void inside of me that I obviously could not hide with the outward accomplishments I was achieving. I really wanted to make the big money but could never seem to get there since I was my best customer.

By the mid-1980s, I watched a lot of friends and schoolmates fall in the drug-and-crime wagon. They either overdosed or went to prison to serve some hard time. That bothered me, but not enough to stop snorting. Cocaine had its deep hooks in me, making me crazy and paranoid. I always worried about getting robbed. I had promised myself that if someone took something from me, they'd get it—and good. One time I suspected my cousin was trying to rip me off, and I hit him so hard he nearly died.

That incident really shook me up and became a personal wake-up call showing me that I was totally out of control. If I didn't find some fast answers I knew I would wind up in the morgue. Although I did not have a personal relationship with God then, I would always talk to Him during my toughest times. In the midst of all these problems I was offered the job of Youth Director of Roxbury Tenants of Harvard.

I felt as if I could offer inner-city young people some help and could develop programs that would enhance their lives. It was a tough job because the organization was located in the same neighborhood where I lived and I was all too familiar with the people who lived there. My mother was actually one of the founders of the organization. I discovered that I had this same desire to help other people like my mother did.

It was there that I met my wife-to-be Michelle. When we met we were both recovering from previous bad relationships. But we discovered that beyond that, we had a lot of other more positive things in common. We started off as "just friends." But two years later, we were married. In fact, my childhood friend, Pastor William E. Dickerson II, performed our wedding ceremony. At the time we were not saved. Michelle and I did a whole lot of things together. Unfortunately one of those things was using drugs. Not the best way to form a life partnership, but I self-medicated to get rid of my anger and pain. And it seemed as if it was doing a good job for me.

In the late 1980s, I took a job at the Mission Hill Community Centers (MHCC), where I developed youth programs. The programs were well received and I moved up to Assistant Director. I vowed to stop using drugs and alcohol. I thought that if I just worked hard enough I could control my bad habits. Trying to medicate my pain from my abuse with drugs just led me to abuse myself in another way by becoming a workaholic. Without drugs, work became my passion. That was all I wanted to do. It became more important to me than Michelle and ended up putting great pressure on our relationship. Still I did not really care enough to make the changes that I so desperately needed.

It was at this time that I again ran into William E. Dickerson II. Dickerson was someone I used to play basketball with in my childhood days. We were basketball teammates on our high school team at Boston Latin School. Unlike me, he had started going to church and had totally submitted his life to Christ. He told me he had started teaching for a living and planned to start a church at the African American Institute at Northeastern University. He wanted my wife Michelle and me to join his church.

We became two of the charter members of the church. I rededicated my life to Christ after joining the church. We started attending Bible study classes at his home and growing in the Word. At the same time, I was offered the Directorship of the Mission Hill Community Center. My career, marriage and church life made me feel as if I'd finally resolved all of my old problems, putting them to a final rest.

Boy, was I wrong. It seemed like problems would occur almost every year from that time. In 1992, my older brother died. He was poisoned on Christmas day. I remember how angry I was that he tried to get a job but couldn't because no one would hire an ex-convict. For no apparent reason my inner circle of friends stopped supporting me in my youth advocacy efforts. Although I had had pain as a child, pain now was introducing itself to me in a totally different way.

Feeling totally jaded by everything that was happening, I resigned from my job as the director of the youth center. The enemy played with my mind heavily. Had this been a few years earlier, I would have turned to drugs to deal with my circumstances. Instead of turning to drugs, alcohol or overworking, this time I turned to the Word of God and actively spent time in prayer. I started working full-time for Dunk the Vote as its founder and director. It is a voter registration/educational organization that I still lead today. It had always been my dream to create my own social activist organization and I considered it a sign of personal growth that I was actually ready to take on such a great responsibility.

During all this difficulty, Michelle and I started experiencing some problems in our marriage that led to separation. This was perhaps the most painful thing that I had to deal with, but I knew beyond any doubt that God had surely delivered me and I could not look backward. So, I again turned to God—this time in a different way because it seemed like there was no one else I could rely on. There was just God and me. I became so close to Him and began to know Him and, in the process, began to learn more of who I am in His eyes. I soon realized that the Lord did not want me to lean on my pastor or my mom during this character-developing time.

Two months later, I got a disturbing call that my father had died. Even though my father and I were not as close as I would have liked us to have been, there was a new sense of loneliness that I felt for the first time in many years. It felt as if there was a void there because of what our relationship lacked. Bothered by that, I took some time off from my work just to organize my thoughts.

Michelle came to my father's funeral and was so supportive. We ended up reconnecting and working on healing our past troubles. As a result, our relationship became better than before. We purchased a home and had a child together. What started dawning on me is that the problems that began to happen in my life after I received Christ were far more substantial than the name-calling and sneering remarks that I received as a child. But this time I was handling my problems with the Word of God, not drugs.

An entirely new world and revelation hit me when I discovered that had I used God's Word from the onset of my problems, I would have been so much further along. The pain of the racial slurs and jeering was nothing in comparison to losing my brother and my dad, yet with God I was able to survive both experiences and come out on top. When I separated from my wife, the love of my life, I knew for sure that I would experience my greatest hurt.

She was one person throughout my life who really accepted me for who I was and did not judge me by the color shade of my skin or the coarseness of my hair. In some ways she gave me a new identity. Larger than all of that, even larger than life itself, was that I had a greater identity, one that my wife, dad or brother could never give me. I had come to realize that I had the image of God. I came to realize this more and more as I would listen to my pastor teach the Word of God and then go home and study it on my own.

Once that truth became resident in my soul, the truth itself became the only treatment that I would ever need. The truth of the matter is that, although I despised how I was treated and how I viewed myself, it doesn't really matter at all. It never should have mattered. My Creator, the One whose image is indelibly printed on my face, will always determine my worth. I was delivered not only from drug addiction and drug selling but more importantly from the other image of myself. Because of that, my life will never be the same just knowing that I look good. Currently I am a deacon at my church, Greater Love Tabernacle, and a political and social activist. Also, I often speak at various schools, colleges and religious settings in regards to leadership development, politics, building God's kingdom through civic participation and more.

Therefore, if anyone is in Christ, he is a new creation; the old has gone, the new has come! (2 Corinthians 5:17).

Toxic Love Nearly Killed Me

Testimony of Minister Renita White

❧

But God demonstrates his own love for us in this: While we were still sinners, Christ died for us (Romans 5:8).

We had what the old folks called puppy love. Back then, I thought it was cute to have someone being so protective of me. I was only 14 years old and Ralph was like a warm blanket always wrapping his arms around me. Our high school friends saw us as the ideal couple. But, what started out as a fantasy ended up as a nightmare. After I gave so much of myself to the relationship, I found myself lost somewhere in the mix. Not knowing where I was, I began to realize this relationship had stolen my identity.

I became this little girl trapped inside a woman's body. At first I thought it was love. But I discovered that what I thought was love was really obsession. Both of us were obsessed with each other and we were too young to know the difference. I learned to hold on too tightly to men before I even met Ralph. It started when I was a little girl. I grew up in a middle class neighborhood with my sister, two brothers and my mother. The image I had of my father was of a man of authority who demanded respect.

Although I was a stranger to my father, my imagination made him so different to me. I remember him picking up my sister and brothers in a big fancy car with a television in the back seat. It was as if he was boasting to a seven-year-old. I knew he loved his car more than he loved me but I imagined that I was his favorite child. My father was so proud of his money and his car. He beamed with excitement and joy over his brand-new Cadillac. I never believed Dad was all that interested in his own children. He then simply faded out of our lives.

I was born in Erie, Pennsylvania. My family and I would return home to Erie to visit extended family for the summers while living in Boston during the year. When I was 14, we lived in a Boston neighborhood. In this neighborhood young boys and girls used to hang out in large groups in front of people's houses. One day when we were hanging out, Ralph passed by. All of my friends were checking him out. I never thought about going out with him because I was only 14 and he was 16. My mother was very strict and having a boyfriend was not on my mind.

Ralph began to ask my friends questions about me. Finally, he got the courage to ask me to sit on his apartment stoop. We began to hang out like the best of friends. The first two of the eight years were the best of times. He treated me with respect and protected me like I was a queen. Despite his kind treatment, my mother refused to accept him. Perhaps it was a mother's intuition or something like that. Ralph would buy me expensive gifts. I never asked or wanted for anything. He just bought them because of his love for me.

When I was in high school, he bought me a $600 bracelet, gold bangles and expensive rings. My mother told me to not accept any expensive gifts from boys. If I would have listened, I could have avoided a lot of trouble in my life. I didn't know he was buying my love. I later realized that those gifts came with a far more expensive price than I was willing to pay.

The first time Ralph hit me I was 16 years old. It was obvious that I was growing into a woman and other boys started to take notice of me. Ralph didn't like all the attention that I was getting. He wanted me all for himself. One night I was hanging out with friends at the local skating rink and came home a couple hours later than usual. Ralph asked me where I'd been. He wasn't my daddy or my husband so I refused to answer him and he slapped me smack across the face. It totally shocked me.

Right then and there, I told him that our relationship was over. He begged for my forgiveness and told me that he loved me. No one had ever hit me before. And I was totally unaccustomed to being physically abused. He knew that he had hurt me pretty badly. Yet, I forgave him and he started to shower me with his love all over again.

During my senior year in high school, I played on the basketball team, ran track, was an honor student and started to model for fashion shows. At 18, I began to prepare for college. Ralph was 20 and working full-time. One night as I was preparing for a fashion show Ralph's jealousy escalated. He was pacing outside my house and yelling that he had to see me. My mother told him to go away but I could still hear the urgency in his voice. I pushed passed her so I could put a stop to his drama.

I only wanted to see him to calm him down. When I came outside and he smashed an egg on my head, my mother said, "I'm in charge here," demanding our attention. "I don't want him around here anymore,'" she said. Ralph looked at my mother liked she'd lost her mind. He stayed on me like a magnet. Everywhere I went there was Ralph, letting everyone know that I belonged to him. The control and abuse got worse. But, I felt like my life would end without him.

He was my blanket of protection. Ralph was the answer to the void in my life. If he left, I'd feel rejected again. I thought about how I felt when my father left and I couldn't handle being abandoned again. I secretly wanted him out of my life if he couldn't treat me like the special girl I once was. But I didn't know how to end the relationship. One night Ralph came back to my house in a rage.

He was yelling for me to come outside. He threw a brick in my window to get my attention. My family and friends had enough. They rushed the door and hit him in the head with a baseball bat, stomped on him, spit at him and chased him away. He still kept calling the house. I thought he was going to die that night. I managed to sneak away from the protective custody of my family so I could see him. He begged me to marry him.

Not thinking straight, I wanted to show him love and to protect him as if he were the victim. A few days later, he called the house and threatened to kill himself. "Go ahead,'" my mother boldly told him. She wanted me to know that Ralph would kill me before he killed himself. He started drinking and taking drugs. I felt like all of this was my fault. "If I can't have you, no one else will have you," he told me. Immediately I thought of my mother's warning. I was in way over my head and it scared me.

Ralph's mom came to my work and had lunch with me. She told me that Ralph's father was very abusive and controlling and it nearly destroyed her life. She wanted me to leave Ralph and to completely cut him off. "Choose life," she warned. I pushed her advice to the back of my mind and focused on my plans to leave for school. I tried to stay busy. Then, fear gripped me. I looked over my shoulder for Ralph everywhere I went.

I would run from my car into the house, expecting that he'd be hiding somewhere to grab me. My fear was grounded in the things Ralph said. He'd call me and tell me my whole schedule for the day. He was watching and manipulating me with his threats of killing me. I hated him for loving me this way. I hated him for being obsessive and controlling. I hated the very thought of him. I no longer wanted him in my life. I wanted to end his life or mine at this point. If I killed myself, I'd be free. But I held on and I just stopped listening and talking to him.

Finally, I went off to college feeling bitter, hurt and wounded. Ralph did not have any idea that I was still living in Massachusetts. After being away for about a year, he finally let go of me; however, I was still afraid of him. I hated the thought of another serious relationship and being in love, so I surrounded myself with a wall of protection. I promised that I would never give all of myself to a man again. It was a rule that I intended to keep.

Two years later, I was still hurt, but I met a nice man named Mike. He showed me love, respect and kindness. With this relationship I was in control. My family and friends thought I had it all, a nice place to live, nice car, a good job and a respectful boyfriend. But it was all a lie. Being so depressed, I hoped someone would trade places with me. I felt very lonely and empty. The void that existed in me was one that Mike couldn't satisfy, or anyone else for that matter. My heart, soul and spirit were thirsting for the love of God.

I was invited to services at Greater Love Tabernacle. I was so distrusting of the strangers around me that I sat in my car in the parking lot during the service and watched the pastor through the window. I told myself that I needed to see what this man was all about. Even though he was well dressed and had a bright smile, there was something that I didn't like about him. I finally gathered the courage to take a seat inside the church.

The pastor reminded me of my father. I wanted to know how he treated his family, so I watched him walk, talk, preach and speak. His words touched my soul. I wanted to know this pastor's God. I left the service, cried in my car and asked God to show me if He was real. I wanted to have the same joy this man of God had. Before I knew it, I was back home, speaking in tongues.

I didn't know about the power of the Holy Spirit at the time. I called my grandmother and she told me, "This is the

Lord's way of communicating with you." I hung up the phone and cried out to the Lord. The next day I went to church and received Christ as my Savior. God spoke to me over the next few days. He told me to leave my relationship with Mike. I told Mike that it was over and he told me that the church was a cult. My family and friends said I didn't need to be saved. I didn't understand completely, but I wanted to be obedient to God.

I was living with fear, anger, mistrust, guilt and shame. I needed God to work on me. I surrendered my life to Christ. He came into my life and revived and restored me. A thirst for the Word of God began to develop in me. The pastor's sermons were instructive. I learned who I truly was in God, how to forgive those who hurt me and how to respect and trust men. It took a long time for me to be comfortable around men, even my pastor. However, God placed me in the right church with the right spiritual father to develop me as a woman of God. I transformed from a dying little girl inside to a bold preacher and teacher.

I have been saved for over ten years now. I thank God for every sermon, revival, Bible study and ministerial class. I can sleep at night with peace. I have joy that the world couldn't give me. I know Jesus Christ as my personal Savior. I have a church that believes in healing, deliverance and restoration. I have a testimony for God's glory and for others to receive the victory.

Marijuana and Alcohol Had Me Bound

Testimony of Pastor William E. Dickerson II

※

Before I formed you in the womb I knew you, before you were born I set you apart; I appointed you as a prophet to the nations (Jeremiah 1:5)

This is my story, the author, William E. Dickerson II. I grew up in the inner city of Boston, Massachusetts. Unlike many kids, I was fortunate enough to live with both of my parents and siblings from the time I was 4 until I turned 16 years old. However, when I was just a toddler I lived very briefly in a foster home with some of my siblings due to my mom's battle with mental illness. (You can read more about my mom's deliverance in her story entitled "The Devil Wanted Me to Kill My Kids" featured in this book.)

Sadly enough my mom died when I was only 16 from complications related to pneumonia and diabetes. My mother was a missionary and an evangelist who taught me to serve the Lord. Because of her profound devotion to the Lord I was upset with God. Due to the weak theology of the pastor, I thought God actually took my mom because the pastor and church members were saying, "The Lord took your mom to live in heaven with Him." This left me emotionally wounded.

The pain lingered for a while until I got saved and came into a more mature understanding of death and the afterlife. As a child, I attended Sunday school and church quite faithfully. My mom used to teach all her children the Bible from a very strict holiness perspective. My dad never said a whole lot, but he was caring and a good provider. Through my mom I learned how to serve the Lord and through my dad's example I was trained to be a responsible young man.

The first time I received Christ, I was eight years old. Due to my lack of knowledge of God's Word I ended up backsliding. When I was 18, I rededicated my life back to God. The time in between those years were some of the toughest days in my life, but I also had much fun. The main vices that I struggled with throughout most of my teen years were drugs and alcohol. From the age of 14 until the age of 18 I used to abuse drugs and alcohol on a regular basis. Although I had a solid family life during most of my formative years, that did not matter at all. My substance abuse problem triumphed over my strong family foundation.

When I was 12 I smoked my first marijuana joint. That same year I also was introduced to hard liquor. As I recall I drank a full glass of scotch and a can of beer. Since I was a novice at drinking, that first time had such a potent effect on me that I became totally out of control. I became very belligerent and wanted to fight my older friends. I was only a kid yet I was so intoxicated that I tried to fight an adult I was drinking with. When I got home that night I literally passed out on the floor. When I had awakened I ran to the bathroom where I vomited in the toilet off and on for nearly 40 minutes.

My mom suspected that I was sick with a virus since the thought of her innocent baby boy being drunk never crossed her mind. As a result of my curiosity I decided to get high off of marijuana (weed) for the first time. At that time I still was young and naïve. I was always the youngest one running with a group of guys who were a few years older than me. In fact, one of my older friends introduced me to smoking marijuana. He lied to me, making me believe that it was his first time getting high.

Sometime later I found out that he had gotten high several times before. He encouraged me and told me that we could experiment together for the first time. After that day of getting high, I started an addictive habit that would last throughout most of my teen years.

Growing up, I was very athletic. I played football and basketball. I was a good ballplayer during my teen years, even when I was high on the basketball court. I did not play basketball while I was high on a regular basis but occasionally I'd get high when I got depressed, to try to ease my depression. However, the majority of my time I would wait until after the game to get high.

From the ninth grade to the eleventh grade, I would get high on the school bus or in the bus station just before I went to school. At least twice a week I would skip class or play hooky from school in order to get high and drink alcohol. From grades 7 to 12 I attended the Boston Latin School. Latin was a prestigious exam school in Boston, Massachusetts. Many of the students after graduation went on to attend Ivy League universities. However, at this same school I witnessed many students of various races smoking weed and drinking liquor on a regular basis. Sometimes they would get high behind certain buildings in the educational and medical district where the school was located. A few students were bold enough at times to actually smoke weed down in the sub-basement of the school. We called it "the dungeon." However, I was not that bold to risk suspension or expulsion. I got used to smoking joints because I felt it was safe. I never would have believed that I could have allowed this casual drug to get the best of me.

When I was high, I felt relaxed, at ease and worry-free. I began smoking not just for extra-social activities, but also to cope with life's problems and trials. The devil made this experience so convenient for me because I often got free marijuana from friends. I got as high as I wanted to as often as I wanted to, sometimes even a couple of times a day. I did careless and irresponsible things while I was high.

Sometimes I got into fights, defied authority figures, disrespected schoolteachers and stayed out until the late hours of the night or even the next day. After my mom died my dad and I were more like roommates than father and son. He provided for me and would speak to me, but my mom's death took such a negative toll on him that Dad became more introverted. Because of that, I did not want to burden my dad with my questions about drugs and sex.

So I turned to get some of life's questions answered from street-smart men who lived in the community. I wanted to fill a void that was created after my mom died, but the responses I received did not help me. I was really seeking to be reconnected to the Lord but I did not realize it at that time. I started socializing more with guys who were used to getting high to cope with their problems. The strange thing about these associates was that none of them actually talked about their problems. I knew there were issues I was dealing with; therefore, I looked at them as being shallow and fake. I was seeking peace within myself, so the Lord would periodically use a Christian to minister to me about my concerns.

During my sophomore year there was an incident where I got high on some marijuana that was tainted with some bad stuff, but I did not know it. That day I stayed high from the start of school until a few hours afterwards. I started having hallucinations while I was in school. I had a severe case of paranoia that came over me during and after school. That day, I managed to avoid most of my teachers and my dad. At one point during that day I thought I was going to die. My chest started hurting and I had difficulty breathing. Scared to death, I prayed to the Lord to deliver me.

God did heal my heart pains, and when I began to feel better, I didn't serve the Lord at all. Senselessly, I continued to abuse various drugs and alcohol. I actually experimented a few times with angel dust. This is a narcotic that makes the abuser have hallucinations and feelings of paranoia. Once, I took this drug around the time that one of my relatives died. I was so high on this drug that it made coping with the death a tougher experience than it should have been.

I started hallucinating and hearing voices. My body started feeling very strange to me. I began to shake and cry uncontrollably. I was alone at the time. No one knew what I was dealing with. I guess it was hard for the adults to see my problems because I was an athlete and a preacher's kid. When the feelings calmed down, I was able to be in the presence of others, but I was still high. For a moment it felt like I was on top of the world, then I crashed emotionally.

Afterward, I was depressed for about a week. Because I was embarrassed at the time I did not seek any psychological help. I was only 16 years old when this situation happened. Although I hadn't totally given up everything, I surely didn't abuse angel dust any more after that last traumatic experience.

When I was 16 years old, my mom died. She was only 48 years of age. This was the worst thing I felt could have ever happened to me. I was sober during the whole funeral arrangements and proceedings. In fact, after my mom was buried, I decided to give my life to the Lord. I guess I had a "crisis salvation" at the time because I really didn't stay true to my commitment to Christ.

I was tricked by the devil to believe that I was too young to be saved. Because I didn't surround myself with other young Christians, I ended up straying away again. At 16, I began to party more and have casual sex to placate my emotional pain. The trauma and pain of my mother's death caused me to have very unhealthy relationships. I started cutting back on smoking marijuana, but I increased in drinking. Drinking hard liquor caused me to act out violently at times.

I was a young man full of anger and pain. The drinking continued until it affected my schoolwork. On a few occasions, I missed school because I had a hangover. Since my mom wasn't around to minister in her motherly way, my dad related to me almost like I was a grown man. He probably figured that he didn't have to worry about me all that much since I was a boy. Many times on the weekend I called my dad and told him that I was going to come home the next day.

He just gave me his consent without even checking to see where I was staying. Don't get me wrong, my dad was a nice man and a good provider, but he didn't talk enough to me about life. I was normally staying the night at a friend's house. My friend's father gave me plenty of free marijuana and alcohol. Sometimes when I went to my friend's house, I would smoke marijuana and drink beer with my friend's dad, an uncle and a few other guys since they purchased it in big quantities. My friend's dad was a drug user and a drug dealer.

A capitalist at heart, he sold marijuana to adults and children in the neighborhood. For some reason, he liked me and was very generous toward me. Therefore I got a lot of joints free of charge. The whole game started to feel kind of comfortable to me but I was cautious. One day a couple of guys I knew got busted by police for selling drugs. When that happened I backed off quickly. I did not mind smoking a joint here and there, but I definitely wasn't going to go to jail over it. Some of my relatives were in prison already. And I knew for certain that was not the road for me. After that, I would still get high at times. Sometimes when I got high, I got into arguments or fights.

111

Once at a party, a few girls were trying to restrain me from fighting a guy waiting outside for me. This guy was so angry at me, until he pulled out a gun and shot a guy twice by mistake, thinking it was me. I thought the situation wasn't about me, but I later found out that it was and that I could have died that very night. God let me escape and to this day I don't know whether the individual who was shot lived or died.

On other occasions I was shot at by individuals while I was in all-white areas (racism was a major overt issue in Boston, Massachusetts, in the 1970s) and once in the hood, but thanks to the Lord, my life was spared again. Though they should have been, the shooting incidents were not turning points in my life. One day I decided while I was high that I would get a gun for my protection. During the 1970s, teens carrying guns was nowhere near as common as it is nowadays.

My sister's boyfriend gave me a gun. I did a little target practice and thought I was ready. Well, one night, my sister's boyfriend borrowed the gun from me and he got arrested. He went to jail for a year. I looked at that situation as God sending me a message. Why wasn't it me? Why didn't I get arrested for possessing the gun? After that, I didn't touch a gun anymore. I thank God I never had to use a gun on anyone in my life.

A major turning point with my marijuana abuse happened when I was at a friend's house getting high. This night, there was a spread of weed on the floor. There was maybe about two or three pounds of weed on the floor and we began to roll joints and to smoke several joints of what was called "Colombian Gold." I got so high that I could not move from my chair.

My brain wasn't sending the correct signals to my body. It felt like I was stuck in the REM stage of sleep. I was convinced I couldn't move and I got scared. I thought I was paralyzed. I ended up falling asleep until the next morning. I awoke about five or six hours later. I vowed to myself that I would never smoke marijuana again. However, I broke my promise on several other occasions after that morning.

In my junior year in high school, I resolved to stop smoking and drinking because I didn't want substance abuse to hinder my basketball skills. I was determined to be successful in basketball. The road to my deliverance from drugs and alcohol was frustrating because of my denial of the problem. When I used my will power to stop abusing substances, it did not last long. For as long as I live I'll always remember that day that I got totally delivered and set free by the power of God: December 26, 1979.

I was alone at home in my bedroom. It was my senior year in high school. Since the start of the basketball season, I was hampered by back and knee injuries. I was not playing up to my full potential. Our team lost the game that day. It was the day after Christmas. I blamed the loss on myself because I took the last shot and missed. I went home angry and disappointed because of the loss. I felt so down that I went straight to my bedroom and began to pray.

I was praying to God to heal my body, but the Lord knew what I needed the most. When I wasn't saved, I would end my prayers by saying, "Lord, one day, save me." After ending the prayer, I heard what I believed to be the Lord's voice say, "Where would you go if you died today?" I honestly could not say heaven. I stood up and the presence of the Holy Spirit knocked me back on my knees. I started crying, coughing and choking as I wrestled against various demonic strongholds. After well over an hour I fell out on the floor and my body got very limp. At that point I realized that I had been set free.

I prayed sincerely and asked Jesus the Christ to save me and to be the Lord over my life. I repented verbally for every sin I could think of at that time. I called my brother Lawrence who was saved at that time and he helped to disciple me in the Lord. I joined a strong, Bible-believing church and have been serving the Lord ever since that day.

Of course I have had many ups and downs in life and every time that I failed God, I kept on moving on. But I never went back to the lifestyle of drugs and alcohol. I maintained my deliverance through keeping the right company, staying in deliverance worship services, fasting and praying and studying the Word of God. And I made it a priority of mine to testify about my deliverance every chance that I got.

If you are battling with substance abuse, I want to encourage you that you too can be delivered. The same God who set me free is here to set you free as well. Today I am married to my childhood sweetheart Luella. We have been married for 24 years and lead a progressive church in Boston, Massachusetts, which I founded in 1989. I have been drug and alcohol free and faithful to my wife for over 24 years. *Jesus the Christ is the Great Deliverer!*

Part Two

Nine Steps to Deliverance

❧

Step 1: Acknowledge the Sin

Sin is progressive. The book of James tells us that when sin is conceived, it brings forth death (1:15). First is desire, or lust, then comes sin, then comes death. Now, lust doesn't have to mean that you just lust after fleshly things or sexual things. A person can lust after drugs, alcohol, money or just about anything that is not of God. Our sins, if left unchecked, will eventually lead us on a path toward spiritual death, which is disconnection from God. We must acknowledge and confess our sins before we can establish a strong relationship with God. Then, Jesus Christ promised in His Word to forgive us of all our sins and to cleanse from all unrighteousness (1 John 1:9).

Acknowledging our sins puts us on the road toward getting help. We need to first admit that we have a problem and refrain from calling our sinful ways a disease. If we don't acknowledge it as sin, we'll continue to stay in hiding and we won't deal with it. God can't heal us if we're covering

117

things up. He can only heal us of what we reveal to Him. Even though He knows everything, He wants us to be honest enough to reveal certain things to Him because He has made us agents of free will.

We will find help when we say to God, "I need help." If we don't say it, we won't seek help. Denying our sins and bad habits just sets us up for running away from deliverance. In that case we lie to ourselves, saying, "I can get over it. I can stop." The truth is that we must earnestly acknowledge our problems so we can deal with them. Otherwise, we'll continue living in the mire of sin.

Functional drug addicts and alcoholics, for example, believe that they are "okay" because they haven't ended up on skid row. They lie to themselves that they can stop. This is denial, not acknowledgment. They won't ever be set free by the power of God until they say honestly to God, "I want help. I want to be free." Acknowledging it means you must confess, "I want to move on with my life. I want to be completely the person God wants me to be." So if you have a sin in your life that is causing you to miss out on the fullness of an abundant life, consider what Jesus said in John 10:10: *"The thief comes only to steal, kill and destroy; I have come that they may have life, and have it to the full."*

So the first step to deliverance is acknowledging our sins. It is as simple as this prayer: "I know that I'm wrong. I want to make things right so that I can bring glory and honor to God's name. I can do what He would have me to do, and I can be the person that He has ordained for me to be." As you do that, you will begin to see that God will give you humility and your prayer will transform you. "Lord, here I am. I have a problem."

Step 2: Confess the Sin

"If we confess our sins, he is faithful and just and will for-give us our sins and purify us from all unrighteousness," the Bible tells us in 1 John 1:9. The Bible also tells us that with-out the shedding of blood, there is no remission of sin (Hebrews 9:22). Because the Lord Jesus Christ paid the price to set us free from all our sins, we boldly and coura-geously confess our sins to the Lord and to all the people we've hurt during our times of sinfulness and unrighteous-ness. Our confession is an act of acknowledging sin, which means we are ready for healing and deliverance.

James 5:16 says, *"Confess your sins to each another."* There are times when we must confess our faults to one another so healing can occur. If we've wronged our brother or our sister, we must confess that wrong before we can be healed and set free. It also helps to pray and ask God for the right time to ask for forgiveness and to seek the assistance of mature Christians who can tell us how to handle our dif-ficult trials.

The Bible also tells us in Romans 8:1 (KJV): *"There is therefore now no condemnation to them which are in Christ Jesus, who walk not after the flesh, but after the Spirit."* In other words, the freedom that God gives us has enough strength to override our feelings of guilt. We should never confess something simply out of guilt. That doesn't help us in the deliverance process. We confess sin because it puts us on the right track for the Lord to set us free.

Guilt is a part of sin, yes, but it only helps us to understand our sin. Real conviction from the Holy Spirit lets us say, "I did wrong. I sinned against God." God delivers us and sets us free when we confess, but that confession has to be from a change of heart, not just because we were caught or have a bad conscience. We will never be delivered if we cover our sin, if we all of a sudden confess because we got caught. No, we must pray, "Lord, help me to hate the things You hate and to love the things You love."

Don't allow the devil to make you feel bad if you fall into sin. There is no condemnation in Christ. Simply ask God to forgive you and move on. He *will* forgive you. He *will* deliver you, but it takes confession. Pinpoint those things that hinder your walk with the Lord, that cause you to live a secretive life, a hypocritical life and an inconsistent Christian life. You can be saved and still be troubled by sin, but if you want to be delivered and set free to go to a higher level in God, you must confess the sin.

The devil likes to hold things over us. But do not fear. Once you tell the devil, "Devil, I am telling God about my skeletons. I'm bringing them out of the closet. Devil, you can't hold anything over me because I'm not worried about being caught. I'm telling on myself so I can be set free," there is nothing further he can do about it.

Keep in mind that if you need to confess to somebody something that you did, make sure that you have everything lined up to deal with any negative ramifications from your confessing to that person.

For example, a couple decided to move to another level in their marriage after going through some frustrating times. They sat down to talk. "Let's air this thing out. Let's really make sure that we can move to the next level. And let's be very transparent and lay all the cards on the table." The husband told the wife, "Well, you go first. You tell me some stuff. Let's lay everything out, move on with our lives and really take our marriage to the next level." The wife replied, "Okay, before we go any further, I want to let you know that I had an affair and was cheating on you." That day the marriage ended. The husband was devastated by the fact that his wife cheated on him (even though he had cheated too but did not tell her). She confessed something that her husband couldn't handle. They weren't prepared for the ramifications.

Confession simply means you want to get it out so you can move on and go toward a place of deliverance and freedom. But if you don't confess, you can't possess. Get rid of the negative things in your life. God will give you greater strength to enhance your walk with Him. Confession is vitally important in your steps of deliverance—for as you confess, the Lord will set you free.

Step 3: Accept Forgiveness

We can't grow if we confess and then do not accept God's forgiveness. We can't move beyond confession without forgiveness. We have to accept the fact that we can be forgiven. Say to yourself, "The Lord has forgiven me." Can you accept that statement?

We also must seek the forgiveness of the person we've harmed. The Bible says in Matthew 18 that if we have ought against our brother in Christ, we are to go and ask that person for forgiveness. If he doesn't forgive us, we should invite a spiritual mediator to help us bring about a peaceful resolution. But we cannot confess our sin and then continue to walk under a cloud of guilt, hurt, frustration, depression or anguish. If the Lord has forgiven us, we need to go and sin no more.

That is what Jesus told a lady caught in the very act of adultery. The men who caught her and brought her before Jesus were ready to stone her. Yet, when Jesus finally responded to them, He said, *"If any one of you is without sin, let him be the first to throw a stone at her."* These men who knew they had problems, had sins, had unrighteousness within them, put down their stones and walked away.

Keep in mind that these men said this woman was caught in the act. So, what were they doing that they caught her? Were they involved in a peep show with somebody being intimate with her? If so, they were involved in sin. Even though we do not commit the sin, but have pleasure in those who do it (either by watching it or viewing it on TV), then we commit sin within our own hearts. Jesus said that if a man looks at a woman to commit adultery with her, he has committed sin within his own heart (Matthew 5:28).

As this woman stood there feeling dejected, ostracized and hurt, waiting for that final sentence of death, Jesus told her, *"Go now and leave your life of sin."* She had to accept that Jesus forgave her and then she had to walk in that forgiveness. (Read John 8 for the full story.)

Do not let anybody put a guilt trip on you or make you live under a cloud of their judgment or scrutiny, for if they really have the love of God in them, they're going to love you to life. Galatians 6:1 says, *"Brothers, if someone is caught in a sin, you who are spiritual should restore him gently. But watch yourself, or you also may be tempted."* In other words, we ought to have the spirit of restoration in our lives and be applying it to other people, letting them know that "if God restored me, He can restore you."

In order to do that, however, we have to recognize that when God forgives us, He forgives us right then and there. He does not wait until later to forgive us. Religious folk will make you feel like God doesn't forgive you right away, that you have to do a whole lot of things to work your way back into God's good grace. God is not like that. He knows how to forgive us and He knows how to set us free from whatever has us down. Psalm 86:5 says, *"You are forgiving and good, O Lord, abounding in love to all who call to you."* So confess the sin and accept God's forgiveness. Go and leave that life of sin.

Step 4: Repent

Once we confess the sin and accept His forgiveness, the next step is repentance. Genuine repentance involves making a total 180-degree turn away from sin and toward the things of God. Understand that godly sorrow is not enough. Godly sorrow works toward repentance. In other words, it is the bridge that brings a person face to face with repentance. When we repent, the Lord gives us strength to let go of the sinful things we have struggled with. After we repent, a change takes place spiritually. That is when we can begin to position ourselves for recovery.

That recovery happens when we position ourselves to be closer to God. We position ourselves so we can walk in liberty. Jesus was sent to earth to teach us about the importance of repenting and receiving the Good News of the kingdom. John the Baptist was His messenger. He prepared the way for Jesus. We must understand that God wants us to renew ourselves by repenting and calling on His Name whenever we are in trouble.

When we repent the scriptural way, we are simply saying no to the evil, negative things and to the sins that had a hold on us. "Lord, I want to serve You; I want You to be my Savior and my Lord." That becomes the cry of the repentant soul. There is an old adage that says, "If God the Father cannot be Lord of all, then He is not willing to be Lord at all." In other words, God does not want us to treat Him like a part-time lover. God is supposed to be supreme in our lives. He is supposed to be the One who rules and reigns and we must give Him our full attention at all times.

The Bible shows us many people who've repented. Consider the story of David. He was approached by Nathan the prophet after he was caught in his sin. David repented once he found out that Nathan had blown his cover. He said in Psalm 51:10, "Create in me a pure heart, O God, and renew a steadfast spirit within me." David recognized that his sin was wrong and he quickly confessed it to the Lord. How did he repent? He repented by turning away from those things that once gripped him and held him in captivity. He allowed himself to be set free by repenting.

It is important to denounce demonic strongholds. Sometimes we willfully want to sin. We may say that sin is in us and that is just how we are. Some folks make the poor excuse that "the devil made me do it." Because we don't see ourselves as being accountable for our own actions, we yield to the desires of the flesh. The devil desires to use our bodies to do evil when God wants us to use our bodies to do good deeds.

One of the titles of the devil is "the prince of the power of the air." When we think of the air we think of the heavens. The first heaven is the physical heaven you see with your naked eye. Demonic spirits inhabit the second heaven, which we do not see. God dwells in the third heaven on the throne. The devil can tamper with our souls when he crosses our communication with God.

After the devil does that, we will be more vulnerable since we will not feel God's strength. Then, if we don't feel like praising God, we won't. If we don't feel like going to church, we'll simply stay at home. Acting on those negative feelings will eventually disconnect our communication with God. So we should persevere through that soulful realm to get to the spiritual realm. Then, the spirit, the part of us that longs for God, will be renewed and recreated in the image of Christ.

One thing that every believer needs to know is that our flesh won't ever be born again. The good thing is that our spirits can be born again. We are actually more spirit than we are body because the Lord made us to be living spirits. This body is going to decay and go back to the dust but our spirits will live on forever.

Once we denounce these demonic strongholds, we start to re-strengthen our spirits and rebuke the demonic strongholds over our lives. If one is living with demons, he or she needs to surround him or herself with people who know how to pray through by casting out the devil. God's Word lets us know that we have the authority to cast out devils. Yes, He has given us the authority to cast out the devil!

Pray this prayer with me right now: "I denounce, in the Name of Jesus, the strongholds of _____ over my life. In the name of Jesus, I am confessing today that I am a child of God and I will do the work and the will of God. I acknowledge that Jesus Christ is Savior and Lord, that God the Father has sent Him into the world to redeem humanity back to Himself, and that His Spirit is yet moving throughout the land. I willingly denounce every demon spirit that has caused me this pain and trauma in my life today. Today, I stand in agreement with God's Word. I denounce every spirit that is not of God and I set myself in agreement with the Lord that I am free, in Jesus' Name."

If the devil has you bound by fear, renounce fear. Maybe the devil has you bound by fornication, pornography or the spirit of homosexuality. Whatever he has had you bound by, renounce it in the Name of Jesus. Turn from what you used to accept as normal behavior and begin to practice walking in the will of God.

Step 5: Pray and Fast

The disciples were confounded when Jesus cast out a demon in a boy after they could not. Why couldn't they help the boy? Jesus answered plainly, in Mark 9:29 (NKJV): *"This kind can come out by nothing but prayer and fasting."*

We use both prayer and fasting when trying to get our breakthrough or maintain our deliverance. Fasting is simply going without food, sometimes water too, for a certain period of time. The Lord might lead you to go on a 24-hour fast. (If under a doctor's care, get permission before fasting.) On a 24-hour fast, we can do without both food and water. But if we fast for more than three days, we should drink some

126

liquids so that we don't get dehydrated, sick or pass out. Fast with wisdom.

The body of Christ engages in many types of fasts. Briefly, there is the Daniel fast, when we eat only certain foods. Perhaps you'll fast from meats, or perhaps you'll eat only vegetables. That is the type of fast Daniel did when he refused to eat the king's delicacies in Babylon. Another type is the normal fast when you go without food for a period of time, but drink water for several days. The absolute fast goes without food or water. Only mature Christians should go on an absolute fast for more than three days. Be cognizant of health issues.

I know from experience over the years that fasting is very beneficial. Fasting helps to bring the flesh under subjection to the Holy Spirit. You see, if we can say no to food, then we can say no to other things. Fasting also gives us humility, and we find ourselves in the presence of the Lord asking Him to have His way within us spiritually.

If we feed our flesh, it will dominate our lives. If we feed our spirits, then our spirits will dominate our lives. So as we fast and go without food, we deny our flesh physical food but offer our spirits spiritual food: the Word of the Lord.

The Lord shows us His love in His Word. He tells us how to walk by faith and not by sight, which is how He operates. Fasting and prayer help to move us closer to the things of God. Fasting is not archaic; it has not gone out of style. It's time for the saints of God to fast because it is something that the Lord wants us to do.

Fasting also allows us to see our spiritual nakedness. In other words, we realize that we're nothing without God. Our prayers expose us when we say honestly, "Lord, I need Your strength to get from this place to the next level." We recognize that our spirits were denied the fruits of peace, love and joy because our fleshly desires took over. We bring those desires to our knees when we yield to God through fasting and prayer. We become vessels that can be used for the glory and honor of God. We become closer to God the more we pray, fast and worship.

God empowers us to fast and pray on an individual level so we can seek the face of God. Then His will is done not just in heaven, but also here on earth. God has given us the keys and the authority to the kingdom. We must release that power and the glory God has placed within us. However, we must put ourselves in the position to receive it. We must fast and pray to be victorious in Christ and mature in the Lord. Then we can walk in the power, dominion, authority and strength of God.

As we mature in God, we increase our prayer time. We never get enough chances to seek God's face. We pray day and night. We say, "Lord, I'll steal away." We commit ourselves to praying as soon as we open our eyes in the morning. Get up seeking His face and I guarantee that you'll see some results happen in your life. Commit to consistent prayer and fasting.

If you are not at that point yet, then just start small. Take the 20 minutes you normally spend eating breakfast, double that time, then devote it to God. Say, "I'm going to fast and pray during this time so I can build myself up and strengthen myself in the things of the Lord." Fasting on a regular basis helps you get to the place where God wants you to be. As you are able, determine to increase your fasting and prayer life and it will become easier. Trust God that you can do it and God will meet you halfway.

God wants us to be strong. He wants us to have the right mind-set to walk in deliverance. Romans 12:1-2 says, *"Therefore, I urge you, brothers, in view of God's mercy, to offer your bodies as living sacrifices, holy and pleasing to God—this is your spiritual act of worship. Do not conform any longer to the pattern of this world, but be transformed by the renewing of your mind. Then you will be able to test and approve what God's will is—his good, pleasing and perfect will."*

Reading the Word of God renews our minds. We have to get that Word in us so our minds can be renewed and we can start thinking like God thinks. The devil tricks us into believing that we cannot walk in deliverance. When he feeds us negative thoughts, we doubt our deliverance. Then we backslide and start getting involved in negative behaviors all over again. But if we put the Word of God in us, we gain greater power and stamina against sin. We stay determined to reach a higher level in the Word of the Lord.

Fasting helps us achieve that higher level in the Word. When we can go without food for a week, we will see our weaknesses. As God ministers to us through His Word, that Word penetrates the cracks and crevices of our spirits, souls, understanding, intellect, reasoning and rationale, and it works some things out of us. That Word cleanses us. That Word washes us. That Word renews us.

Hebrews 4:12-13 says, *"For the word of God is living and active. Sharper than any double-edged sword, it penetrates even to dividing soul and spirit, joints and marrow, it judges the thoughts and attitudes of the heart. Nothing in all creation is hidden from God's sight. Everything is uncovered and laid bare before the eyes of him to whom we must give account."*

We study the Word so we can learn more about living a victorious life—not just when you go to church, but when you are on the job, at school or surrounded by people who do not love you or the Lord. The Bible has so many stories of successes and even failures that we can learn from. It can help to mature you so you can be the son or daughter He ordained for you to be.

And although this is not specifically related to prayer and fasting, let me also mention that you must establish a spiritual devotion, such as praise and worship at home, to keep you grounded. Praise reveals the glory of the Lord. Everything that has breath praises God, according to the psalmist. But worship is for those who are in covenant with God, those who are in fellowship with God. Those who are in right standing with the Lord can worship Him in the beauty of holiness.

Praise and worship is like warfare. Don't just praise Him when things are going well; praise Him when things are bad. Believe me, every time you praise and magnify God in the Spirit, He shows up!

The more we praise and bless God, the smaller our problems and trials appear. The pressures of life don't seem as great. Why? Because as our praise goes up, the strength that God has for us comes down. And when we get that strength, we can go forth and walk in the deliverance that God has for us.

Here's an example of praise. Say, "Lord, I glorify You, for You are the One who has delivered me. And I worship You because You are the Lord of Lords and the King of Kings. I worship You, Lord, because You are the One who is able to sustain my deliverance. I worship You, Father, because You're able to give me the strength that I need for this day."

Praise and worship the Lord everywhere—as you do chores at home, while driving in your car, etc. When you do that, the devil has no place to get in your life! He has no place to get in because you're surrounding yourself with worship. You're surrounding yourself with the glory of God.

Therefore as we praise Him, we begin to worship Him on a new level of intimacy because we have a spiritual connection with our Father. We honor and adore Him for who He is. We trust Him to maintain our deliverance. We do not walk by what we see; we walk by whom we know. Panic is not what we do. Running is not what we do. No! Praise is what we do! When problems come, when trials come, when faced with uncertainties, when the devil sends bad thoughts, when the devil tries to entangle us in bondage again, praise is what we do.

So as you praise and worship the Lord, as you get in His Word, as you pray and fast, the devil has to back up! James 4:7 says that when we resist the devil, he flees. That word *flee* in the Greek means that he runs in terror!

Step 6: Be Filled with the Holy Spirit

Ephesians 5:18 says, *"Do not get drunk on wine, which leads to debauchery. Instead, be filled with the Spirit."* It is important that when a person who has been inhabited by demons or been demonically influenced for years is delivered, he or she needs to be filled with the Holy Spirit.

131

Many people believe that the sign of being filled with the Holy Spirit is speaking in tongues. Although I agree that it is a sign, it's not the only sign. I believe that another sign of being filled with the Holy Spirit is having and displaying the fruit of the Spirit, as recorded in Galatians 5:22-23. Either way, by being filled with the Holy Spirit we are saying, "Lord, I want You to be in control. I don't want to be in control. I do not want to sit on the throne of my life dominating things and calling the shots." In other words, we're telling God that we want Him to lead, guide and direct us.

To be filled with the Spirit means that we submit to the Lord's will. We submit our ways to the Lord's ways and allow the Holy Spirit to take up residence in us in a greater manner. You see, we received the Holy Spirit when we got saved, but being filled with the Spirit is a greater move of God. Being filled means we have gone to another level of maturity, insight and illumination.

It is important to be filled with the Holy Spirit so that we can maintain the previous steps of deliverance and not give place to the devil. We also need the infilling of the Spirit so we can flow in the Spirit. In other words, there are spiritual gifts that belong to us, and if we are not filled with the Holy Spirit, we won't be cognizant of how God wants to use us at that particular level. But as we yield to the Spirit in us, those gifts will flow out of us.

Then take your prayer life to another level by being saturated. Forget your expectations and start living up to His expectations. That is what I do. I want everything God offers. Whatever God has in His Word, I want every bit of it. If it is speaking in tongues, I want it. If it is prophesying, I want it. If it is laying hands on the sick, I want it. I want all that God has for me. In fact, being filled with the Holy Spirit is critical to maintaining our deliverance because the Holy Spirit helps us to be more sensitive to what is going on in the spirit realm.

We often speak of being filled with the Holy Spirit as the "baptism of the Holy Ghost" or the "baptism of the Holy Spirit." (The words *Holy Ghost* and *Holy Spirit* can be used interchangeably.) When we are baptized in the Holy Spirit, we exhibit certain signs of that infilling. For instance, when we speak in tongues and flow in the spiritual gifts, then we become a greater witness for the Lord. That last one is an important reason for being filled with the Holy Spirit, as recorded in Acts. When we receive the explosive, dynamite power of the Holy Spirit, we have to go out and witness and win souls to the Lord.

When the disciples in the book of Acts were filled with the Holy Spirit, they went out and witnessed, sharing their faith with others, and the church began to grow. As we are filled with the Holy Spirit, God empowers us to be a witness for Him. He empowers us to open up our mouths and talk of His goodness.

We also are more sensitive to the Holy Spirit when we are filled with Him. That means we are not going to walk in sin. We are not going to walk in willful disobedience. If we do, we have removed ourselves from the realm of allowing the Holy Spirit to direct us, rule us, govern us, where He takes pre-eminence in our lives.

It is critical that we allow ourselves to be filled with the Holy Spirit to sensitize ourselves to the spiritual warfare that we are engaged in. With the Holy Spirit in us, we can under-stand the tricks and the strategies of the devil and how the devil maneuvers and operates. We want to make sure that we don't allow any demons of the past to return in our lives. If demon spirits do come and try to reattach themselves to us, we want them to say, "We tried to get in, but the Holy Spirit was there."

To be filled with the Spirit means to have Him occupying every area of our spiritual house. That means no room is left unoccupied for some demon to think it can go in there and live. Born-again believers cannot allow the enemy any foothold into our lives to cause us to do the things he wants us to do. That includes things that please our flesh and are demonically inspired.

For instance, if we say we are not going to curse anymore yet cursing comes out of our mouth, then we have not allowed the Holy Spirit to control that area of our lives. If we say we are not going to lie anymore, but let some slip, then we have not allowed the Holy Spirit to be dominant in our lives. As a result, the devil gets a foothold and begins to operate on what came out of our mouth.

What does the Holy Spirit do for us if we are filled with His power? The Holy Spirit empowers us to be a witness. He reveals the things of God to us; He leads us and guides us into all truth. He impacts every area of our lives that we submit to Him; the Holy Spirit moves us to a level of greatness in God. So understand that God wants us to be filled with the Spirit. He wants us to do great works for Him. But we must have the power of the Spirit in order to do that.

Step 7: Be Accountable to a Mature Christian and Receive Christian Counseling

Many people are hindered from maintaining deliverance in their walk with God because they haven't sought help from a close friend, associate or minister whom they can confide in. They need someone who will help them and not condemn them, someone who won't kick them to the curb or tell their business to somebody else. Confidentiality is very key and vital when seeking deliverance from sin. Look for someone who knows how to keep his or her mouth shut.

It is important to be accountable to a mature Christian and receive Christian counseling. How do you find a mature Christian to help you? Here are some characteristics. A mature Christian is one who knows how to build somebody up when he or she is torn down and how to speak positive things when someone is caught up in negative things. A mature Christian has a handle on the Word of God and knows how to use it. Such a person has a deep relationship with the Lord, and that relationship with the Lord has caused him or her to rise from some pain he or she previously experienced. This Christian is honest, walking in integrity at all times; he or she is not a man-pleaser but a God-pleaser in all that he or she does. A mature Christian knows that one of the main priorities in life is to win souls unto God and has wisdom from up above.

So when you find this mature Christian, you need to check in with him or her on a daily basis. Why? Someone who has received deliverance needs another person to ask him or her, "How did your day go?" As you grow in the Lord, you don't have to meet with that person every day. But it is still important to have that relationship so you can keep a handle on your victory. No matter what demonic influence you were freed from, such as alcoholism, drug addiction, fear or depression, you must be able to go to somebody whom you can talk to and share these things.

That person is the support base, not a crutch, because he or she is mature enough to let you know when you are wrong, are slipping or are getting weak again. That mature Christian will help to guide you in the right path. Although that Christian may not be a trained counselor, he or she should be strong and able to help, pray with, study with and guide you in the things of God.

At times some people need solid Christian counseling. I know a young gentleman who years ago had this saying: "I don't counsel people. I just cast the devil out of them and they are free." Sometimes a person might not have a devil but still need counseling. Not everything pertaining to habits and sin is caused by demonic bondage. Sometimes it simply is part of the pleasure of things we like to do, and we need to bring those things under the subjection and the power of the Holy Spirit.

Christian counseling helps us to see when we've been hurt in the past and have baggage. Mephibosheth, in the book of 2 Samuel, sat at the king's table because David showed kindness to him. Yet, Mephibosheth was crippled because he was dropped as a young child. Some of us have been dropped, and it is not because we have a demon. For instance, I have known people who were molested as children and never overcame it. The pain they felt stopped them from enjoying the intimacy of marriage. A lot of those people weren't possessed by demons. They simply needed Christian counseling in order to deal with their pasts.

We see people who have been "dropped" on our jobs, in our schools and even at church. A good counselor can find out why that person acts the way he or she does. A good spiritual counselor can gradually learn to identify the individual's personality, habits, family background and the events in that person's life that led him or her to the juncture where he or she seeks deliverance.

We all have key people in our lives who encourage us as well as those who stress us out. Others may try to distract us from our faith. They will do anything they can to get us off the track God has put us on. God wants us to go forward, but there are some people who are definitely a hindrance to that. Eventually we get broken down physically and mentally. We must deal with people who give us stress and who try to distract us. Our counselors should help us through the pain. And as we deal with the pain, we will know how to go through whatever hurt, pain, anguish or disappointment that comes against us.

Not everyone needs to see a psychiatrist. The difference between a psychiatrist and a psychologist is a psychiatrist can prescribe medication while a psychologist or a counselor cannot. Some folks might need medication to help get them balanced. Their troubles might not be caused by demons. Some people deal with chemical imbalances in their body; some might have a bipolar disorder. We don't classify them as having a demon. Let them know they can get help. The same God we serve has given wisdom to doctors. So there are certain isolated situations where people might need a medication to help treat their mental health problems.

At the same time, if Christian counseling is going to be effective, it must remain true to the Bible and depend on the Bible as the guidebook, the ultimate book of reference.

I know there are a lot of different approaches to counseling, like psychoanalysis, client-centered therapy, a Rogerian approach (based on Carl Rogers who taught others to counsel people), Adler, or even methods that Sigmund Freud employed through psychoanalysis. I believe that we must stay true to the Bible, but we can use other sources as references to help us in receiving the counseling we need.

Stay true to the mature Christian you are accountable to and receive great instructions and advice from your Christian counselor. If you need a counselor today, call your pastor or New Life Christian Counseling at 1-800-NEWLIFE for the name of a good Christian counselor who can help put you on the path toward deliverance.

Step 8: Stay Away from Negative Influences

It is crucial, in order to maintain deliverance, that one stays in the right environment and around the right influences to keep the freedom one received by the power of God. In 2 Corinthians 6:14-17 we are told, *"Do not be yoked together with unbelievers. For what do righteousness and wickedness have in common? Or what fellowship can light have with darkness? What harmony is there between Christ and Belial? What does a believer have in common with an unbeliever? What agreement is there between the temple of God and idols? For we are the temple of the living God. As God has said: 'I will live with them and walk among them, and I will be their God, and they will be my people.' 'Therefore come out from them and be separate, says the Lord.' "*

When the Lord sets us free, He sanctifies us. It is a process that God does within us. Sanctification simply means that we are separated unto God for His use. We are not just separated from the world, but we are separated from the world of sin based on purpose. God has a greater purpose for us.

When God told the children of Israel not to intermarry with the surrounding nations, it was not about ethnicity or race. Rather, it was about God protecting His children from polytheism—the worship of many gods—and idolatry. We don't want to be influenced by those who are worshipping the gods of money, fame and material success. We are to be the light of this world and the salt of the earth. As light and salt, we make a difference by shedding light on the darkness.

We must always be careful of the company we keep and the places we frequent. If hanging out at nightclubs was what brought you down and caused you to get into drugs and illicit sex, you can't casually go to nightclubs. That is not the right place for you to be. When we get delivered from drinking alcohol, we cannot be around social drinkers. We will get caught up. Social drinkers can take a few sips and go home, and everything will be fine with them. But alcoholics need to stay clear of alcohol and of hanging around people who drink alcohol on a regular basis.

If your sin or your problem or your habit was pornography, you can't find yourself going to R-rated movies where the women are wearing scant dresses or bikinis and there are nude scenes. Those things will stir you up. You have to learn how to starve your eyes. (If this is your struggle, I recommend a good book for men entitled, *Every Man's Battle* by Stephen Arterburn and Fred Stoeker.) Sexual immorality can be a strong demon and a strong spirit. It is very important for us to stay clear of those things that bring us down and cause us to lose our strength. Just as Delilah deceived Sampson and Sampson's strength was zapped. Every man must stay clear of a Delilah spirit and people who are promoting the Delilah spirit. That is a seducing spirit that will cause us to go under.

The Bible tells us in 1 Corinthians 6:18, *"Flee from sexual immorality. All other sins a man commits are outside his body, but he who sins sexually sins against his own body."* So, we must cut those unhealthy soul ties when we are delivered. To remain free, we must continue to walk in the freedom that God has given us. We cannot allow ourselves to be entangled again with those yokes of bondage. We must stay clear of anything that could cause us to lust after pornographic images.

Also, stay clear of the Jezebel spirit. This is the spirit of witchcraft that often people ensnares people. Jezebel was a wicked woman who dominated her husband and hunted down the prophets of God to kill them. She wanted total control. We must get as far away from this spirit as possible, especially if we've had problems with people manipulating and controlling us in the past. (John Paul Jackson wrote a good book about dealing with the Jezebel spirit, *Unmasking the Jezebel Spirit,* which gives us a better understanding of the topic.)

Just staying away from negative influences is not enough, however; we must replace negative friends, associations and environments with positive people and places. We need to surround ourselves with mature Christians who are spiritually minded—not carnal Christians who are always cracking off-color jokes and jesting about things that are not edifying to the spirit. Get around Christians who talk about the Word of God and the importance of prayer.

Sometimes we need to be with "deep people"—those who are just focused on prayer and the Word of God. They don't have time for a whole lot of social mumbo-jumbo; their focus is on building up themselves and others in the Word of the Lord. Get around mature Christians who'll speak life-changing words into your spirit. Find people who know how to put the Word of God and prayer in the forefront of everything they do.

My wife and I got married when we were quite young. I was 19 and she was 17. We were sustained during our early years because we stayed around spiritual-minded people who often spoke the Word of God. We gathered at their homes at times in prayer. We did not use our youth as an excuse to sin or to yield to the flesh.

It was very important for me and very relevant for me to be around men of integrity. It helped me throughout the duration of my ministry to be a man of integrity, to stay away from situations that would bring shame to the Gospel of Jesus Christ and profane the Name of Jesus. Rev. Dr. Samuel Hogan, my spiritual leader and pastor at the time, was very important to me. I stayed in that church faithfully for ten years before the Lord sent me out to be a pastor. He taught me to be a man of integrity. I was able to stay focused in the Lord as I traveled the country because I had a good leader guiding me.

If we surround ourselves with mature Christians who can help build us up, as we maintain healthy relationships with mature Christians, we will be led in the paths of righteousness and will maintain our deliverance.

Step 9: Testify About God's Power of Deliverance

Once we find deliverance, nothing stops us from testifying to what God has done for us. Revelation 12:11a says, *"They overcame him by the blood of the Lamb and by the word of their testimony."* We might testify in a church setting, during a one-on-one conversation or in a group. I was taught that when you stand up and give a testimony, you first give acknowledgments to the leaders, the pastor and his wife for instance, and give glory to God. You honor man, but you glorify God. Second, use a scripture that relates to your testimony. Third, testify about the goodness of the Lord in your life, what the Lord has done and how the Lord has brought you out of your trials.

Never allow your testimony to turn into a "boastimony." Oftentimes people will boast in their flesh about the great things they have done and will kind of say what the Lord has done through them, but they will actually be boasting, not testifying.

Other times we can go overboard and give too much information in our testimonies. People don't need to know all the details of our sins and our past experiences. Yes, they need to know that the Lord saved you and set you free, that the Lord delivered you from drugs. But they don't have to know that you had a $500 a day habit and what you used to do in order to support that habit. Know the difference between enough and too much information. Let the Lord speak to your heart concerning what you need to share and how to share it because, in our testimony, we can sometimes implicate other people who do not have the opportunity to share their side of the story. I have heard people testify in churches using the real names of people: "I ran with so-and-so; I hung with so-and-so." Don't use your testimony to indict anybody. Don't use your testimony to glorify any negative past experiences.

Instead, testify about God's deliverance. This ninth step is just as important as the first when testifying to others about God's power of deliverance. God delivers us to become tools. He needs us to win souls for His glory and honor. Our testimony should be a means of bringing others closer to God, not bringing them closer to us. We don't testify to win people to ourselves. We share the goodness of the Lord so others can see the power and the glory of God. We must stand up and be counted because, in the book of Romans, Paul tells the church in Rome, *"I am not ashamed of the gospel, because it is the power of God for the salvation of everyone who believes"* (1:16). We testify because the Lord does not want us to be ashamed. If we deny Him down here, He will deny us when it really counts.

We must always glorify God, always talk well of our heavenly Father, always talk well of our experience in the Lord, always talk well of the church. Yes, it is vital that we speak well of the church, even within our testimony. Sometimes we make the mistake of speaking to sinners about negative things that have transpired in the church since we have been saved. As a result, we have hindered them from coming into the family of God because of our negative testimony.

Our testimony should bring people to Christ and add to the church. It is important that we share what the Lord has done for us and how the Lord has brought us out of sin. And, yes, at the right time you might use details to share. The testimonies shared in this book were told to glorify only God. These souls shared intimate details about their lives in order to let people know they were set free from what looked like impossible situations. But when you get up and give a public proclamation about what God has done, do not use it as an opportunity to talk about what the devil has done.

We are witnesses of what the Lord has done within our lives. So therefore, we testify to others about God's power of deliverance. It doesn't matter how low we've sunk in life because of drugs, low self-esteem, alcohol or abuse. Regardless of how much sin has inundated your life, you must understand that God's power of deliverance is here to set you free. And as God has set you free, you must walk in that freedom, that victory, that strength.

We must walk in the strength of God's anointing. We don't testify on our own strength, our own power, our own righteousness. We testify because the Lord has given us His righteousness, we are in right standing with Him, we are justified. And because we are justified, we can testify of the goodness of the Lord and tell others what the Lord has done. So in your testimony share the life-changing Gospel, how the power of the Holy Spirit and the love of God transformed your life and delivered you from habits, delivered you from sins, delivered you from a reckless lifestyle. And as you testify, the people who hear will come into a place of being set free by the power of God.

Now, I encourage you, regardless of what has happened in your life, put God first, stay true to the Word of God and follow these Nine Basic Steps for Deliverance. Maintain your deliverance. No matter what your walk of life, ethnic background, or sinful background, be encouraged! I have seen deliverance for myself. I have witnessed the glory and the power of God transform lives. Therefore I can say with great confidence, *"You too can be delivered!"*

About the Author

꧂

Pastor William E. Dickerson II is one of Greater Boston's most influential, socially active and innovative pastors. Born in Newport News, Virginia, and reared in Boston, MA. He is the founding pastor of Greater Love Tabernacle Church. The church has grown into a multifaceted ministry with an intentional purpose of bringing deliverance to the captives from various social, economic and ethnic backgrounds.

William is a national and international conference speaker. He ministers on such topics as deliverance, leadership development, apostolic authority and men's issues. He has been a guest on television and radio programs in the United States and abroad. A man of the letter and of the Spirit, William has earned a diploma in Biblical Studies, a degree in Business Management, a M. Ed. in Counseling/Psychology and a M.A. in Pastoral Counseling. He is a former public school teacher as well as a former college instructor. An exemplary role model and father, he has been married to his wife, Luella, for 24 years. He is the proud father of two sons and two daughters.

More You Too Can Be Delivered

❧

People like you who have been delivered by the hand of the Lord submitted all the stories that you have read in this book. We would be honored to have you contribute your story to future editions of *You Too Can Be Delivered*. Please feel free to send us your typewritten story about how God personally delivered you. We would be glad to consider your story for future publications. Each story will be verified for authenticity and truth worthiness. Send your story of no more than 2,000 words to:

You Too Can Be Delivered Project
101 Nightingale Street
Dorchester, MA 02124

Or email us at WDickerson7@aol.com.